BLUE
SCOTLAND

MOLLIE HUGHES

BLUE
SCOTLAND

The Ultimate Guide to Exploring Scotland's Wild Waters

BIRLINN

First published in 2022 by
Birlinn Limited
West Newington House
10 Newington Road
Edinburgh
EH9 1QS

www.birlinn.co.uk

Map on p. 17 copyright © Helen Stirling
(www.helenstirling.com) 2022.
Contains Ordnance Survey data
© Crown Copyright and database
right 2022.

Every effort has been made to ensure this
book is as up to date as possible. Some
details, however, are liable to change.

The activities featured in this book contain
an element of risk. The author and publisher
cannot accept responsibility for any
consequences arising from the use of this
book. For more details on safety, see p. 207.

Maps featured in Blue Scotland are for
illustrative purposes only. For specific locations,
please consult the OS map, as suggested.

ISBN: 978 1 78027 744 8

British Library Cataloguing-in-Publication Data
A catalogue record for this book is available
from the British Library

Design and typeset by Mark Blackadder

Papers used by Birlinn are from well-managed
forests and other responsible sources

Printed and bound by PNB, Latvia

CONTENTS

Welcome to Blue Scotland 10

Blue health 12

Being a well-rounded adventurer 14

How to use this guide 15

Important notice and warning 16

Map 17

LOCATIONS

Edinburgh and surrounds
Cramond Island 20
Wardie Bay 22
Fidra Island 24
Belhaven Bay 28
Coldingham Bay 30
South Queensferry and the Bridges of the Forth 32
Kinghorn Loch 36
Loch Ore 38
St Andrews 40

Glasgow and surrounds
The River Clyde 46
Canals of the Central Belt 50
The Kelpies 52
Loch Lomond 54
Loch Long 56
Loch Ard 58
Lake of Menteith 62
Loch Awe and Kilchurn Castle 64
Grey Mare's Tail 66
Loch Ken 70

West Highlands
Loch Maree 74
Eilean Donan Castle and the Three Lochs 78
Loch Shiel and Glenfinnan 80
Loch Moidart and Castle Tioram 82
Arisaig Skerries 84
The Ardnish Peninsula 88
Loch Morar 90

Inner Hebrides

Slate Quarries, Easdale Island   94
Fidden Beach, Mull   98
Eas Fors Waterfall, Mull   100
Calgary Bay, Mull   102
Iona   104
Tiree   106

Outer Hebrides

Vatersay   112
Castlebay and Kisimul Castle, Barra   116
Traigh Eais & Traigh Mhor, Barra   118
The Prince's Strand, Eriskay   120
Peter's Port, Benbecula   122
Hosta, North Uist   124
Scolpaig, North Uist   126
Sollas, North Uist   128
Scarista, Harris   130
Luskentyre, Harris   134
Huisinis, Harris   136
Traigh Mheilein, Harris   138
Traigh Ghearadha, Lewis   140
St Kilda   142

The North

Achmelvich Bay   148
Scourie Bay   152
Durness   154
Strathy Bay   156
Thurso East   158
Dunnet Beach   160
Whaligoe Steps   162
Loch Ness   164

The North-east

Bow Fiddle Rock   170
Sandend Bay   174
Hell's Lum, Cullykhan Bay   178
Aberdeen City Beach   180
Stonehaven and Dunnottar Castle   182
Lunan Bay   186

Central Highlands

Loch an Eilein   190
Loch Morlich   192
Loch A'an (Avon) – Cairngorms National Park   196
Linn of Tummel   200
Soldier's Leap   202

Adventure planning & safety

Safety basics   207
Tides   209
Scotland's Outdoor Access Code   211
Responsible and sustainable adventuring 213
Final thoughts   215

Acknowledgements   217

Index   219

WELCOME

WELCOME TO BLUE SCOTLAND

I grew up almost as far from Scottish blue spaces as you can get on mainland Great Britain. Until I was 18, I lived on the south coast of Devon in the seaside tourist hub of Torbay. But growing up there, with its crescent-shaped bay and its hilltops, from which you can look out to the horizon and the ocean, I was always connected to the bigger picture – to the rest of the world, and the wildlife that inhabits this blue space, its currents and swells.

When I was 13, we moved to a house close to the beach. When the wind blew strongly from the east, huge swells would enter the bay; on days like this, you could hear the roar of the ocean from my garden. The bedroom I shared with my sister overlooked the bay and if you were up early enough you could watch the sunrise over the ocean to the east. I think it was at this point in my life that I truly fell in love with the sea. I would spend hours marvelling at its changing moods – usually whilst I was meant to be doing homework or revising for exams. It was also around this time that I started surfing, heading further down the coast with my brother and dad to a beach called Bantham, or, when time allowed, to the north coast of Cornwall, for the bigger swells.

After I graduated from university, adventure took me far from the ocean, far from my small town in South Devon and far from sea level altogether. When I was 21, I joined an expedition to climb Mount Everest from the south side via Nepal. I had been climbing mountains for almost five years by this point and had spent my student loan on trips to far-flung mountain ranges around the world. I studied the psychology of Everest climbers for my final-year dissertation project at university before quickly deciding I didn't want to just write about this mountain but experience the whole journey for myself. After a year of agonising training and sponsorship-hunting, a nine-day trek into base camp and six weeks acclimatising on the mountain itself, I finally reached the top of the world on 19 May 2021, alongside my Sherpa guide Lhakpa Wongchu.

When I returned to sea level, it took a while before I wanted to see another mountain again, but at 23 I moved to Scotland and began exploring this wonderful country from the tops of its highest mountains to its countless lochs and paradise-like islands.

Expeditions continued to take me far from Scotland's shores, but I always returned with a smile, knowing that this rugged and wild country was home. In 2017, having just about forgotten the suffering of my first Everest expedition, I returned to the mountain, this time to climb from its northern Tibetan side. This route felt colder, windier, much more remote and much more technical. After another two months of acclimatising, my small team – consisting again of Lhakpa Wongchu Sherpa, with the addition of British guide Jon Gupta and Nepali Lila Tamang – reached the summit alongside me on 16 May. I became the first English woman to summit Everest from both its north and south routes, as well as, at the time, the youngest woman in the world to achieve this feat, at the age of 26.

A couple of years later, I took on my biggest expedition to date: I set out to ski from the edge of the Antarctic continent to the Geographic South Pole, a distance of over 700 miles. And I wanted to do this solo: no teammates, no guides, and unfortunately no Lhakpa Wongchu! It took me 58 lonely days to complete, during which time I experienced some of the worst weather on our planet, including huge windstorms gusting up to 50 knots, eight days straight of white-out where I couldn't see more than a metre in front of my face, and temperatures down to minus 45°C with windchill. All the while, I was skiing uphill, pulling my 105-kilo sled, which I nicknamed Boudica.

I finally reached the Geographic South Pole on 10 January 2021 and entered the Guinness World Records by becoming the youngest woman to ski from the edge of the continent to the pole, at the age of 29. During these 58 days alone, I learnt so much about myself and what I am capable of, about

the wild spaces on Earth and the fact that we are just visitors to this planet. We need to do everything in our power to enjoy it and preserve it.

I now spend much of my time as a motivational speaker, sharing stories from my expeditions. I am also one of the directors of an ethical adventure company called Ocean Vertical. We take folk on adventures into the oceans and mountains of Scotland, whilst doing all we can to protect this country's remarkable wild spaces. I am an ASI paddleboard instructor and love nothing more than teaching people the key paddling skills. In 2020, I was given the honour of being asked to become the first female President of Scouts Scotland and to support this amazing organisation in preparing young people with skills for life, including a whole lot of adventure.

While researching and collecting photography for *Blue Scotland*, I had the opportunity to spend a year travelling to every corner of the country, exploring first-hand its mind-blowing blue spaces. The book's photographer, Rachel Keenan, and I, often alongside our partners and various friends, travelled from the far reaches of Scottish territory, such as the incredible St Kilda archipelago, situated in the middle of the Atlantic Ocean, to inner-city blue spaces, including a sightseeing tour down Glasgow's historic River Clyde. The diversity of

natural spaces Scotland has on offer still feels somewhat incomprehensible to me; the east coast differs so much from the west, even though they are separated by a matter of miles. Both are raw and captivating in their own ways.

Aside from the natural spaces, what inspired me most about this journey was the sheer number of small-scale, unassuming community-led projects dotted across the country, focusing on protecting the natural environment. Projects such as the installation of toilet facilities in beauty spots, funded solely by the efforts of locals; the presence of information boards linking travellers to the local wildlife and history of an area; the presence of waste disposal units to help avoid the littering of our green and blue spaces; and the community initiatives to protect damaged sand dunes and machair across the islands. Local small-scale environmental activism does work, and it is incredibly motivating to see so much of it across Scotland.

Please use this book as an inspirational guide to explore some of Scotland's wild blue spaces, please marvel at Rachel Keenan's stunning photography, and please do get planning your own adventures to embrace all that this incredible country has on offer.

Mollie Hughes

BLUE HEALTH

I am looking out over an endless blue horizon, with the sound of breaking waves on the shore, the rush of adrenaline when the first icy wave breaks over my head . . . I have always needed blue spaces. I am drawn to them when things get tough; they are a place to find some headspace, to be present, to explore and connect with the natural world.

For generations, people who have engaged regularly with blue spaces – be it via swimming, paddleboarding, surfing or simply walking alongside a body of water – believe them to have a psychologically restorative effect on the mind. They are often places of sanctuary and places to unwind.

The concept of 'blue health' is an emerging topic of study. There is a growing body of research that suggests outdoor blue spaces, which include the coast, lochs, riverways and canals, can have a huge benefit to people's health.

Research has now unearthed evidence to support these beliefs – that there are significant benefits of time spent close to and in blue spaces for people's mental health, general well-being and physical activity levels. The health benefits of time spent in green spaces are now well known and accepted; it is becoming widely accepted that the benefits of blue spaces may even outweigh those, in terms of reducing negativity and stress, as well as inducing a positive mood. It is now proven that bodies of water can have a psychologically restorative effect.

Scotland is famed across the world for its blue spaces: the country has so much to offer in terms of its rugged coastlines and pristine beaches, its endless riverways and deep lochs surrounded by towering mountains.

The Coast

Scotland's 11,000-mile coastline wraps around the west, north and east of the mainland, as well as circumnavigating Scotland's countless islands. The west of Scotland is characterised by the scarring of deep inlets up and down the coast. These sea lochs break up this mountainous terrain. The west coast is also home to the majority of Scotland's outlying islands; the Inner and Outer Hebrides are scattered over this far-reaching Atlantic shore.

In comparison, the north coast is shorter, wilder and more remote, open to (and at the mercy of) icy North Atlantic swells. Off Scotland's frigid north coast lie Orkney, whose extensive sea cliffs are visible on a clear day, and roughly 100 miles to the north-east of the mainland, the remote and wild Shetland Isles.

The east coast of Scotland is characterised by towering sea cliffs in constant battle with the power of the North Sea. Along this coastline you'll experience long open stretches of sandy beach, quaint fishing villages, small towns and three of Scotland's largest cities, Aberdeen, Dundee and the capital, Edinburgh.

The Lochs

Aside from sea lochs, Scotland is also home to 31,000 freshwater lochs. These range from small lochans to gigantic bodies of water – around 350 of them are of notable size. Freshwater lochs can be found throughout the country, from the southern Borders to the tip of the north coast, with the largest concentration being found in the Highlands. The most internationally recognised must be Loch Ness, which rose to fame in the 1930s after the first alleged photos of the infamous monster hit the newspapers. However, there is a lot more to Scottish lochs than mythical beasts; these vast bodies of water, along with Scotland's rivers, contain 90 per cent of the UK's fresh water, an incredibly vital resource for the whole ecosystem.

The Rivers

Snaking across the country, linking bodies of water to one another and the ocean beyond, are the lifeblood of Scotland, its riverways. Covering more than 7,000 miles, Scotland's rivers and streams range from slow, trickling Highland burns to the vast, fast-flowing rivers of the Lowlands. The longest river in Scotland is the Tay, which flows from its source on Ben Lui for more than 100 miles to the Firth of Tay on the east coast.

The Canals

Scotland is also home to an extensive canal system, which covers more than 130 miles of navigable waterways. This includes the famous Caledonian Canal, which slices Scotland from west to east, providing a navigable channel across the country through the mighty Great Glen, and the Forth & Clyde and Union Canals, which connect Edinburgh and Glasgow.

BEING A WELL-ROUNDED ADVENTURER

Scotland is an adventure playground for watersports enthusiasts. With so much variety in its blue spaces, you can literally do it all here. This book covers four main watersports: paddleboarding, kayaking, surfing and wild swimming. Entering blue spaces in Scotland is very much at the will of the weather conditions, the mood of our oceans and the water levels of our rivers. What I suggest is that being a well-rounded adventurer means that more conditions will be right for you to soak up some of Scotland's blue spaces – there are a multitude of ways to access the water depending on the day. Often if the ocean is too calm for surfing, it could be good for paddleboarding. If it is too windy for paddleboarding, it could be good for sea kayaking. If your location is too inaccessible for carrying a kayak to the water, it could be good for wild swimming.

Paddleboarding

Paddleboarding is the world's fastest-growing watersport. It has boomed in popularity over recent years. Paddleboarding gives you a new perspective on blue spaces – from your lofty position standing on your board, you can command your waterway, seeing far into the distance and deep into the water beneath your feet. Scotland has a magnitude of great places to paddleboard, from its coastlines to its fresh- and sea-water lochs, its riverways and its canal systems.

Kayaking

Sea kayaking is a wonderful way to cover large distances carrying everything you need for a day trip or even a week's camping expedition. You can leave the crowds a long way behind and discover the hidden beauty of the Scottish coastline as you move silently through nature, experiencing wildlife up close and undisturbed while exploring hidden coves, cut-off beaches, remote inlets and caves you can only discover from the water.

Surfing

Surfing is one of the purest forms of enjoying a blue space. It involves catching and riding a breaking wave that has travelled across an ocean to crash on our shores. This sport has its origins in ancient Hawaii but began to gain popularity in Scotland during the 1960s along the east coast. There are countless places to surf on the mainland and the islands, from gentle beach breaks to world-renowned reefs.

Wild Swimming

Swimming is potentially the simplest form of engaging in a blue space. Very little equipment is needed, even though wetsuits and tow floats are often recommended. This sport has exploded in popularity during the last few years across the UK – who doesn't know someone who has taken up wild swimming recently? Scotland is an incredible place to swim, from high-level lochs in the Highlands to stunning beaches along our coastlines, and riverways gently flowing out of the mountains en route to the ocean.

HOW TO USE THIS GUIDE

Blue Scotland is primarily an inspirational guide to some of my favourite blue spaces in Scotland. Use this book to help you plan your own adventures – be it surfing, swimming, paddleboarding, kayaking or simply soaking up the blue-health benefits from the shore.

In order to maximise the value you get from this book, I have included definitions for a few of the key phrases that I have used to categorise each experience. You will find these ratings and definitions on each location page.

Activity

The watersport activity that can be undertaken at a location when conditions allow. Includes swimming, surfing, paddleboarding and kayaking.

Experience level

A rating out of five to describe the level of experience you will need to undertake a certain route or enter a certain environment. The higher the experience level, the more time you should have spent honing your skill for the specific activity – and for these levels you should have undertaken the appropriate professional course.

Environment

The type of body of water on which an adventure is undertaken.

Carry time

How long it takes to walk from the start point to the water's edge, based on a moderate pace and carrying a paddleboard, surfboard or kayak.

Public transport

Here will state if public transport is available from the nearest large town or city.

OS map

The Ordnance Survey map number for each adventure location.

IMPORTANT NOTICE AND WARNING

Blue Scotland is a guide designed to provide information on watersport locations in Scotland and is not a substitute for your personal skills, knowledge and experience. In any watersport activity, there is an element of personal risk and risk to property.

Before you go out on any of these trips, you need to consider your skill level and have the ability to control your craft and rescue yourself in the environment you choose. It is recommended that you take watersport training classes with qualified organisations and individuals to gain the appropriate knowledge about safety, planning, tides, weather, personal skills, kit and the environment you will be entering.

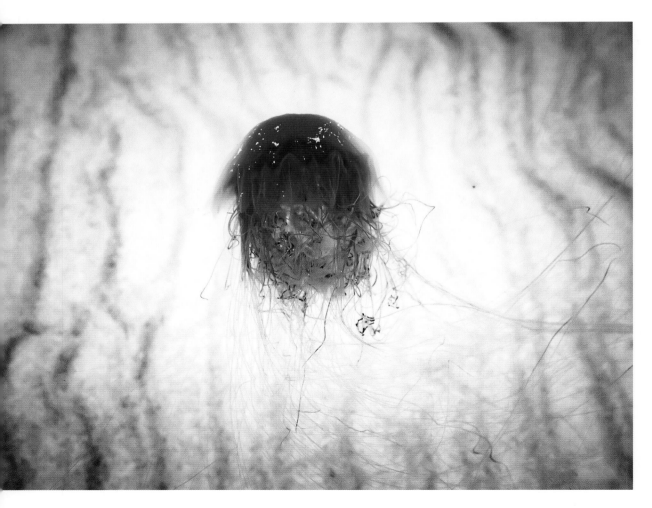

Fair Isle

Orkney Islands

Pentland Firth

Durness • Strathy Bay • Dunnet Beach
Thurso East •
Scourie Bay •
Wick ○
Traigh Ghearadha •
Whaligoe Steps •

Lewis

OUTER HEBRIDES

Stornoway •

Achmelvich Bay •

THE NORTH

Traigh Mheilein •
Huisinis •
Luskentyre •
Scarista •

The Minch

Loch Shin

Ullapool ○

St Kilda •

Sollas •
Scolpaig •
Hosta •

Harris

Loch Maree •

Bow Fiddle Rock •
Elgin ○ Sandend Bay • Hell's Lum •

North Uist

Peter's Port •

Portree ○

Benbecula

South Uist

Inverness ○

THE NORTH-EAST

Skye

Eilean Donan •

WEST HIGHLANDS

Loch Ness •
Aviemore ○
Loch Morlich •
Loch an Eilein • Loch A'an (Avon) •

Aberdeen Beach •

Barra

Prince's Strand •
Eriskay
Traigh Eais & Traigh Mhor •
Vatersay • Castlebay •

Mallaig ○ Loch Morar •
Arisaig •
Ardnish •
Loch Moidart •
Loch Shiel •

CENTRAL HIGHLANDS

Stonehaven •

Coll

Fort William ○

Soldier's Leap •
Linn of Tummel • Pitlochry ○

Lunan Bay •

Tiree •
Calgary Bay • Eas Fors •

Mull

Loch Awe •

Loch Tay

Dundee ○

Iona •
Fidden Beach •
Easdale •

Oban ○

Perth ○

St Andrews •

INNER HEBRIDES

Jura

Colonsay

Loch Ard •
Lake of Menteith •

Loch Ore •
Stirling • Kinghorn • Fidra Island •
Kelpies • Cramond • Belhaven Bay •
South Queensferry ○ Wardie Bay •
Edinburgh ○ Coldingham Bay •

Loch Long •

Islay

Loch Lomond •
Canals •

Glasgow •
Clyde •

EDINBURGH & SURROUNDS

Arran

Firth of Clyde

R. Clyde

Ayr ○

GLASGOW & SURROUNDS

Grey Mare's Tail •

North Channel

Dumfries ○

Newcastle Upon Tyne

Stranraer ○

Loch Ken •

Solway Firth

Belfast ○

0 ———— 50 km
0 ———— 25 miles

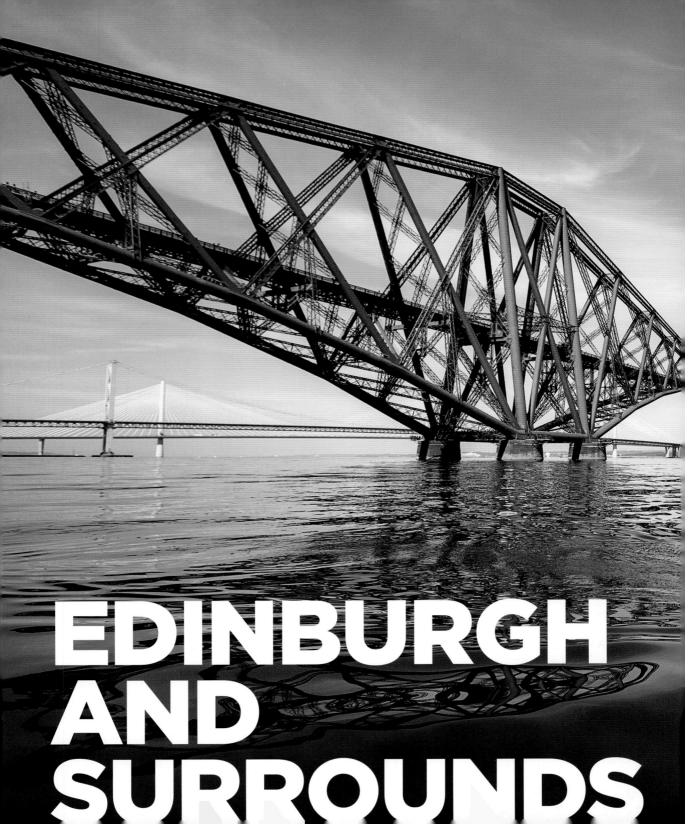

EDINBURGH
AND
SURROUNDS

CRAMOND ISLAND

Activities	Paddleboarding, kayaking
Experience level	✱ ✱ ✱
Environment	River
Start point	Cramond beachfront
Carry time	10 mins
Public transport	Bus connections from Edinburgh city centre
OS map	350

Cramond Island is less than a mile long and consists of 19 acres of uninhabited land. Its highest point is 68 metres above sea level and, from this unique 360-degree vantage point, you can look back at the city of Edinburgh, across to the Kingdom of Fife and up the Forth estuary to the famous Forth bridges.

As a tidal island it is only accessible, to most people, by foot at low tide. Tourists and locals alike have a short window to explore the island and walk back to the mainland before the sea rises and they, potentially, get very wet. However, while the landlubbers are restricted to the mainland, us paddleboarders and kayakers have the opportunity for an adventure. Cramond Island is waiting for us during the high tide and a circumnavigation is a relatively short trip with

the feel of a much bigger adventure.

There is ample parking along the road beside the Boardwalk Beach Club; alternatively, you can park in the Cramond beach car park at the most westerly end. Here you will find public toilets, as well as cafes and ice-cream stalls dotted along the shore.

I would advise starting your paddle to the island an hour or two before high tide. Once the tide turns, water rapidly drains out of this area and leaves behind a whole lot of mud, near impossible to wade through with a board or kayak. Additionally, the tide combined with the natural flow of the Forth can make for a strong current and a challenging paddle against the flow.

If you are in the mood for a little more adventure, you could head further upriver to explore the shoreline of the Dalmeny Estate. From this watery

perspective, you get fabulous views of the impressive Dalmeny House and Barnbougle Castle, as well as the opportunity to explore a few quiet sandy beaches.

If for some reason you have ditched the paddleboards for the day and choose to walk over to Cramond Island, there is an easy tool for you to check when it is safe to do so. You can text the word CRAMOND to 81400 to get safe crossing information texted directly back to you by the RNLI.

Unfortunately, it is all too common for visitors to get stranded on the island with the rising tide, so plan your journey well and avoid any expensive and unnecessary call-outs from the emergency services.

This island paddle is reasonably accessible for competent paddlers who are confident in reading a tide timetable. But this trip gives the feel of a much bigger adventure when you are alone on the island at high tide looking back at the sprawling city of Edinburgh from your quiet island retreat.

WARDIE BAY

Activities	Swimming, paddleboarding, kayaking
Experience level	✷ ✷
Environment	River
Start point	Lower Granton Road
Carry time	2 mins
Public transport	Bus connections from Edinburgh city centre
OS map	350

Sitting between the ports of Leith and Granton, to the north of Edinburgh's city centre, is a small sandy stretch and a wee slice of urban blue space. Wardie Bay is no more than 100 metres wide, and it certainly lacks the seaside holiday vibe of nearby Portobello beach, however this quaint space has its attractions, and is a draw for local paddleboarders and wild swimmers alike.

A long breakwater extends 800 metres around Granton Harbour, where you will often see anglers casting off their fishing rods and walkers strolling along on sunny afternoons. This breakwater creates great protection from the prevailing south-westerly wind at Wardie Bay and in turn creates somewhat calmer conditions for paddling and swimming in the sheltered waters close to the breakwater wall.

In recent years Wardie Bay has become a real hub for wild swimmers from Edinburgh – on a favourable day, you will see dozens of people, young and old, wetsuits and skins, entering the water. Even on a less favourable day you are still likely to spot one or two brave souls taking a dip. Many head in

for a quick dunk, while others clad in wetsuits, swim caps and safety floats head out to take a lap of the nearby buoys. There is a wild swimming group that regularly meets here and a very friendly, welcoming vibe both in and out of the water.

In terms of paddleboarding, it can be a great beginner-friendly venue on a calm day. When I bought my first paddleboard, Wardie Bay was in fact the place where I headed to test it out. I pumped up the board on the small grassy area above the beach and to my utter embarrassment I didn't set the valve correctly and all the air escaped very noisily – we have all been there, right?

From Wardie Bay you can head west up the Forth towards Cramond beach and island (see page 20), on to the Dalmeny Estate and even the Forth Road Bridges (see page 32), if you have the energy. Wardie Bay lies on the Firth of Forth, so do be aware of tides: water moves very fast in and out of the firth with the rise and fall of the tide. Always aim to swim on a rising tide; when paddleboarding, keep a keen eye on the wind speed and direction. Additionally, this can be a busy shipping lane at times, so whilst swimming wear a brightly coloured hat and/or tow float in order to make yourself known to other water users.

Access is very straightforward. Wardie Bay is on Lower Granton Road, where there are bus stops and limited parking outside the colourful cottages that line this stretch. Access is through a gap in the sandstone sea wall opposite the breakwater.

At first glance Wardie Bay may not look like much, but the growing community of enthusiasts who use this small space for their dose of blue health is intriguing and alluring. The local knowledge abounds, and the friendly atmosphere makes for a great urban blue space.

FIDRA ISLAND

Activities	Paddleboarding, kayaking
Experience level	★ ★ ★ ★
Environment	Ocean
Start point	Yellowcraig beach car park
Carry time	10 mins
Public transport	Bus connections from North Berwick to Dirleton
OS map	351

One of my favourite spots on the East Lothian coast is Yellowcraig, which lies 3 miles west of the seaside town of North Berwick. This expansive, sandy beach is a real gem and a popular spot for Edinburgh residents to escape the city on a warm summer's day. During the training for my 2019 South Pole expedition, I spent countless hours dragging car tyres up and down this beach to replicate the sled I would be pulling in Antarctica – all the while wishing that I was on the water with my paddleboard

instead! However, the real paddleboarding adventure at Yellowcraig lies 300 metres off the shore.

Fidra Island is an RSPB nature reserve and home to several species of nesting seabirds, including puffins, guillemots, razorbills and even a peregrine falcon. It is claimed that Robert Louis Stevenson's famous book *Treasure Island* was inspired by Fidra; he visited the island several times, it is thought, with his father, who was involved with the building of

Fidra's iconic lighthouse. For well over a century, this lighthouse has been warning sailors off the treacherous rocks that surround the island.

A circumnavigation of Fidra is an exciting but committing expedition which can be taken on by paddleboarders and kayakers. Conditions need to be near perfect, with minimal wind and swell. With this in mind, this trip should be reserved for those with more experience.

Once the island is reached, you can paddle around it in either a clockwise or anti-clockwise direction, depending on the wind and swell. It is always advisable to reserve the easier paddle for the homeward journey.

On the north side of the island there are several small, sheltered bays, perfect for a short rest or to observe the seabirds and resident seals. Do bear in mind that, as an important nesting site for many seabird colonies, it is advised not to land on the island or get too close to the cliffs where birds are nesting. Keep your distance and simply observe the wildlife in its natural environment.

Once the mainland is hidden from view by the island and the true extent of the bird life on Fidra is revealed, you begin to understand how amazing this wee island is. It feels remote, enchanting and wild.

This is an awesome small expedition with the feel of a big adventure, just a stone's throw from North Berwick and within easy reach of Scotland's capital.

BELHAVEN BAY

Activities	Surfing, paddleboarding, kayaking, swimming
Experience level	*
Environment	Ocean
Start point	Linkfield car park or Shore Road car park
Carry time	10–15 mins
Public transport	Bus connections from Dunbar town centre
OS map	351

The rugged and rural East Lothian coastline extends from the edge of Edinburgh down to the Scottish Borders. Dotted with quaint seaside towns and villages, hidden coves and extensive sandy beaches, its unspoilt beauty makes it a haven for those seeking a dose of blue health.

When I first moved to Scotland from Devon, I was searching for a surfing beach within easy reach of Edinburgh; somewhere I could surf before work or visit to enjoy the long Scottish summer evenings. Belhaven Bay was the perfect spot. This beach lies about 30 miles east of Edinburgh and is an easy drive down the A1. Belhaven Bay is one of the most consistent surf beaches on the East Lothian coastline, picking up even the smallest of summer swells. It's a popular spot with locals, tourists and those (like me) wanting to escape the capital. When the swell isn't rolling in from the North Sea, Belhaven Bay can be a great place for wild swimming on a warm summer's evening. An awesome paddleboarding or kayaking journey can be taken between Belhaven Bay and Dunbar harbour, along an area called Long Craig Rocks, where you can weave in and out of the rocks and islands at low tide.

Belhaven Bay sits within the John Muir Country Park, a spectacular wildlife habitat made up of salt marshes, extensive sand dunes, pine woodland and, of course, golden stretches of beach. The park is named after the conservationist and explorer John Muir, who was born in Dunbar in 1838. John Muir

lived in this seaside village as a child and no doubt his love for wild spaces began as he explored the beaches, forests and estuaries of Dunbar and its adjacent coastline. At age 11, John Muir and his family emigrated to the United States, where his life's work protecting wild spaces across the pond began. It is quite humbling to enjoy the glow of his legacy as you walk through the salt marshes and sand dunes with your surfboard tucked under your arm.

There are two main parking areas to access Belhaven Bay. The first is Linkfield car park, adjacent to East Links Family Park. Here you will find a large paid parking area with toilets and even an outdoor shower, perfect for washing off boards and wetsuits after a surf. There is also a very cool-looking kids outdoor play park next to the toilet block. It looks to be the type of place I would have loved as a kid before I was interested in the ocean! From this car park you can follow one of the many faint paths through the salt marshes and sand dunes to reach the beach – wetsuit boots or wellies are advised, unless you like the squelch of mud between your toes.

The second parking area is in Belhaven village itself. It is a smaller paid car park on the ocean side of Shore Road, opposite the Belhaven Surf Centre. From here, you can cross the Biel Water to get to the beach; at low tide, take 'the Bridge To Nowhere' across the inlet. This famous bridge gets its name as at high tide only the bridge remains visible above the water, with no access to or from it.

In terms of surfing, checking the condition of the waves before committing to the water at Belhaven Bay is notoriously tricky. From each car park, the line of sight to the waves is blocked or too far to see, so you often don't know its quality until you are

dressed in your wetsuit, squelching through the mud, listening out for the roar of the ocean, but by this time you are committed and most likely going to get wet, whatever the waves are like.

This beach has a friendly vibe in the water. It is often used by local surf schools and on smaller days there are usually lots of beginners out honing their skills. Belhaven Bay is a huge expanse of beach, with multiple peaks along the water and plenty of waves to go around. It is popular with SUP surfers and you will often see a few out on a good day.

Belhaven Bay is within easy reach of the capital and has great facilities close by. The backdrop of the striking Bass Rock and the power of North Sea swells give this beach a wild and rugged feel.

COLDINGHAM BAY

Activities	Surfing, paddleboarding, kayaking, swimming
Experience level	✴ ✴
Environment	Ocean
Start point	Car park opposite St Vedas Surf Shop
Carry time	5 mins
Public transport	Bus service from Berwick-upon-Tweed to Coldingham village
OS map	346

Ten miles north of the English border, along the Berwickshire coast, lies the historic village of Coldingham. To get to the water, pass this quaint wee village, with its history stretching back to the seventh century, and follow the minor road past the caravan park. Coldingham Bay soon opens in front of you. Here you will find a stretch of glorious golden sand, charming multicoloured beach huts lining the shore, and rocky outcrops flanking each end of the bay. Coldingham is one of my favourite destinations on the east coast to surf, paddleboard, swim or simply soak up the sea air on a coastal walk.

There is a large car park directly opposite the St Vedas Surf Shop; disabled parking is found further down the hill, conveniently close to the sand. The surf shop is a brilliant asset to this area, as there are very few of them along the east coast. Pop in to rent a surfboard, pick up some wax or grab a coffee and some local knowledge from Steve, the shop owner who is a keen surfer. Steve also runs regular surfing lessons at Coldingham Bay, repairs broken boards and even shapes new ones.

Another key differentiator between Coldingham and many other Scottish beaches is that it is patrolled by RNLI lifeguards during the summer

months. At present there are only eight RNLI lifeguarded beaches across Scotland, making it a great place for families to visit.

For the best surfing conditions, Coldingham ideally needs a big northeasterly swell to reach this sheltered bay and for that reason it isn't quite as consistent as other surfing locations along this coastline. But on the best days, when the swell does arrive and the offshore wind blows from the west, this beach break provides some great left- and right-handers, and is as good as almost anywhere in Scotland. However, it's important to be mindful of strong rips at Coldingham on big swell days.

I have never found Coldingham Bay to get particularly busy in the water. It lies almost 50 miles from Edinburgh and there are plenty of good surfing spots between the two locations that tend to absorb a lot of the crowds.

When the swell drops off and the sun shines, Coldingham Bay and the surrounding coastline can be incredible to explore on a paddleboard or in a kayak. Turning north out of the bay, you soon reach the small fishing village of St Abbs, with its picturesque harbour and small rocky islands to explore. For the more adventurous, pushing further north you will paddle through the St Abb's Head Nature Reserve, with dramatic cliffs that are famed for their seabird colonies.

The stretch of coastline from Eyemouth to St Abb's Head, incorporating Coldingham Bay, has been of interest to marine biologists, scuba divers and snorkellers for decades. Its clear waters, incredible underwater scenery and unique mix of marine life all add to its appeal. In 1984, the local community established the Berwickshire Marine Reserve to protect these habitats and ensure responsible use of the coastline.

From Coldingham Bay itself, incredible ocean wildlife can be seen. Personally, I have only ever seen massive grey seals popping up to scare me whilst I sit on my surfboard. But if you are interested, have a chat with the locals in the surf shop about the wildlife: huge pods of bottlenose dolphins occasionally enter the bay, and even minke whales come to visit this beautiful blue space.

Coldingham Bay is an incredible place to enjoy via surfboard, paddleboard, kayak or by simply swimming. This beach is accessible for all abilities and has some great facilities, while maintaining its protected, wild beauty.

SOUTH QUEENSFERRY AND THE BRIDGES OF THE FORTH

Activities	Paddleboarding, kayaking
Experience level	✷ ✷ ✷
Environment	River
Start point	The Binks car park
Carry time	5 mins
Public transport	Bus connections from Edinburgh city centre
OS map	350

Floating along under the Forth Bridge and looking up at its iconic red steel structure is a dizzying experience. The sheer size of this bridge makes you feel incredibly small, and when you consider this alongside its history and renown, somehow you feel even smaller.

There are not many human-made structures that fill me with awe and wonder – I am most inspired and mesmerised by the natural world; I could sit and stare at a mountain landscape for hours – but the Forth Bridge is an exception. Its intricate structure, rusty red gleam and its iconic heritage draw you to it. Many times I have caught glimpses of this bridge while driving across its counterpart, the Forth Road Bridge (or, more recently, the Queensferry Crossing), but experiencing this iconic

feat of human engineering from the water on my silent, human-powered paddleboard was incredible.

Rachel and I met on a surprisingly warm April lunchtime to paddle the Forth Bridges for the first time. We grabbed the last available space at The Binks car park next to South Queensferry harbour and pumped up the boards in the sunshine. On the west side of the harbour there is a small sandy beach, which made an ideal spot to launch from. Carrying our boards down to the shoreline, we dodged springtime sunbathers and were soon floating on the water.

The Firth of Forth is very tide dependent, and the water can pull surprisingly fast up and downriver. The best time to paddle out to the bridges is at slack tide, when the water is unstressed, with no movement either way in the tidal system. The Firth of Forth is also a busy shipping area, with countless fishing vessels, ferries, recreational boats and the occasional monster tanker too, all using this small water space. It is advised to keep relatively close to shore, be as visible as possible and stay well away from the shipping lanes.

Our launch point was directly in between the

Forth Road Bridge and the Forth Bridge, so we initially turned left, heading upriver towards the road bridge and its upgrade, the new Queensferry Crossing.

This may be a little confusing to non-locals, I know, so let me break it down. Over this small stretch of water are three magnificent bridges linking South Queensferry to North Queensferry, the capital of Edinburgh to the Kingdom of Fife. The most westerly bridge here is known as Queensferry Crossing and was opened in 2017, a modern and innovative bridge whose fan-like design stretches across the Forth. The central bridge is the Forth Road Bridge, opened in 1964, and now primarily used for buses, cyclists and pedestrians. And finally the gleaming red bridge to the east is the Forth

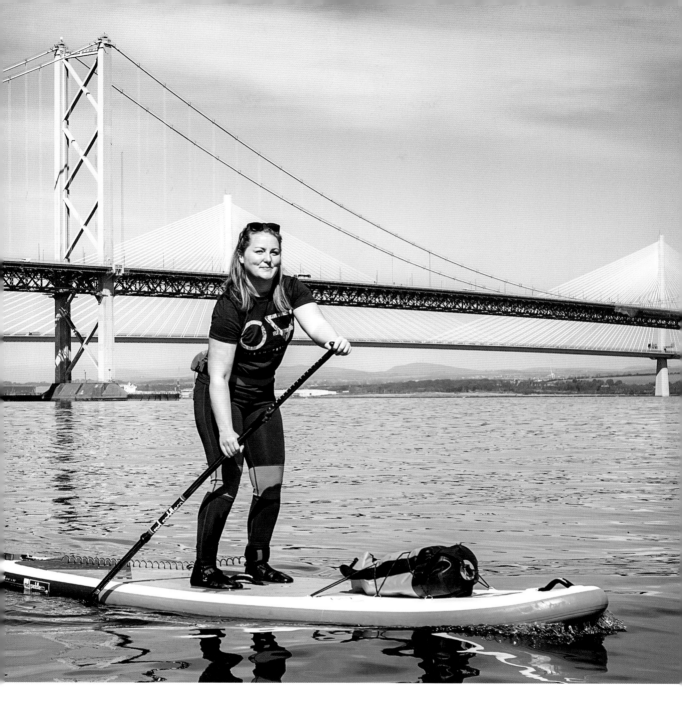

Bridge, often known as the Forth Rail Bridge. Opened in 1890, it is recognised the world over for its engineering fame.

After briefly exploring the two more modern structures, we turned our paddleboards downriver towards the open ocean and the iconic Forth Bridge. Floating under this famous steel structure is a truly awesome experience. Being able to observe its intricate design up close from the water instead of the land is the highlight of this unique paddle adventure.

The Bridges route offers a great slice of blue space a short distance from Scotland's capital. This is an awesome journey by paddleboard or kayak that all local and visiting paddlers should experience.

KINGHORN LOCH

Activities	Swimming, paddleboarding, kayaking
Experience level	✴
Environment	Freshwater loch
Start point	Car park below Craigencalt Farm
Carry time	Lochside parking
Public transport	Train station in Kinghorn town
OS map	367

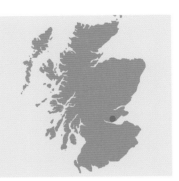

Deep within the rolling hills of southern Fife and a short distance from the sea, you will find the tranquil Kinghorn Loch. A brilliant spot for wild swimming, paddlesports and Sunday strolls, this loch is used and enjoyed by many local groups.

In terms of geology, Kinghorn Loch is relatively young, even though it was formed at the end of the last ice age between 13,000 and 15,000 years ago, as the ice sheet retreated away from the coast. In comparison to other Scottish lochs I have swum in, this body of water is quite small, covering just 27 acres, with a maximum depth of around 12 metres.

Kinghorn Loch is primarily a wildlife conservation area, with an array of nesting birds calling this small sanctuary home. Therefore swimming and paddling in this loch needs to be done with the utmost respect for the wildlife. It is asked that recreational water users avoid the south and west banks of the loch and launch from the small training jetty, not the main jetty, as birds tend to congregate and sometimes nest in this area.

Kinghorn Loch has not always been so abundant

with wildlife. In the mid-twentieth century this body of water was a desolate place; there was a distinct lack of plants, birds and fish. In fact, the only organisms to survive were midge larvae and algal blooms – a very bleak thought indeed! Between 1954 and 1983, Kinghorn Loch was slowly contaminated by seeping water from a local red mud landfill site, killing all the plant and fish life.

This loch had been a haven for wildlife for thousands of years until the impact of humans affected its basic chemical make-up, destroying this habitat. However, like almost all man-made problems, humans also have the power to repair them. At Kinghorn Loch, a lot of work has been put into the removal of the seepage and to improve the water quality. Barley straw rafts were created to treat the blue-green algal blooms and I am pleased to report that the water quality is now deemed excellent. If the sheer abundance of animal and plant life doesn't tell you this, the loch water is also regularly tested and the space is used by many local watersports groups.

Access is straightforward. Directly below Craigencalt Farm you will find a small lochside car park backed by old stone buildings with red iron roofs and pretty blue doors. On the water's edge you will see the jetties from which to launch your

board or swim. There are also often buoys out in the water to aim for when you are swimming or paddling. From this car park you can also access a few woodland trails and picnic areas to keep the family happy while you go for a swim. If you head up to the farm you will find a lovely cafe to warm up in after a dip in the loch, with excellent coffee and cake. There are also toilet facilities located here.

Kinghorn Loch is an accessible, beginner- and family-friendly place to swim or paddle, made more epic by considering its ancient ice age history and the care that has gone into creating this sanctuary over the recent decades.

LOCH ORE

Activities	Paddleboarding, kayaking, swimming
Experience level	*
Environment	Freshwater loch
Start point	Main beach or parking areas along the shore
Carry time	Less than 5 mins
Public transport	Bus connections from Edinburgh and Perth
OS map	OL 57

Situated in a peaceful slice of countryside at the heart of the 1,200-acre Lochore Meadows Country Park, Loch Ore is a good dose of blue health within a built-up environment. Close to the town of Lochgelly and the busy M90 motorway, the park is a real hub for outdoor activities in Fife.

There is a large free car park next to the visitor centre, with toilets, a cafe, an adventure playground, golf and more. It's a great spot for families, with lots of activities to occupy young people, and an entry-level watersports environment.

The beach adjacent to the car park is the perfect place from which to launch your paddleboard or kayak. Once out on the water you can quickly glide away from the hustle and bustle of the shoreline and find peace on the water.

Loch Ore is home to three large islands. The first can be reached quite easily from the beach area,

while the other two require a little more paddle power. Dense woodland makes up most of the islands, with beautiful reeds extending down into the water. There is a wealth of bird life here – you can hear much chattering in the trees, a lovely sound to help tune out the hum of the M90. As with most loch islands, they are best observed from the water to avoid disturbing the wildlife.

Loch Ore is a very accessible place to paddle, the shallow waters close to the beach offering the perfect spot for a beginner's first steps into paddleboarding or kayaking, or a space to hone your paddling skills. The facilities at the country park mean that I'd recommend this as a great space to head out with younger paddlesports enthusiasts. Adventure is easy to find, with trips out to explore the various islands and lots of wildlife to observe. It is a beautiful slice of blue space within rural Fife.

ST ANDREWS

Activities	Paddleboarding, kayaking, swimming, surfing
Experience level	✱ ✱
Environment	Ocean
Start point	Various locations
Carry time	Short (location dependent)
Public transport	Multiple bus connections into town centre
OS map	371

Nestled into the East Neuk of Fife, St Andrews is a small town with a big history. Although it may not be the most famous for watersports, its three beaches (East Sands, West Sands and Castle Sands) show that there's a lot more than golf on offer in this corner of north-east Fife.

My first foray into watersports in St Andrews was surfing on East Sands Beach. The water is very easily accessible from the car park, which can be found just past the Sailing Club on Woodburn Place, where there are public toilets also available. Nearby is a play park for younger members of the family and an excellent toastie shack, which I can personally recommend for warming up after a surf.

I had heard mixed reviews of this break prior to my visit, and the reports of a wave that was best surfed on a mid, rising tide certainly turned out to be true. I'd recommend avoiding high tide, if possible, as the waves get very dumpy.

However, on a day with an offshore wind and a north-east swell, St Andrews is a brilliant spot, as is evidenced by the crowds of surfers who arrive. Rarely in Scotland do you meet such a diverse group of people on their boards in the water. Locals who have been surfing the Scottish coast their whole lives mix and trade tips with students who have come from all over the world to study at the University of St Andrews.

On a flat day St Andrews offers up a wonderful spot for paddleboarding or kayaking. I would recommend launching at East Sands and heading out round the pier towards Castle Sands. At high tide you will often see folk jumping off the pier into the sea – a great adrenaline rush for those brave enough! I would, however, advise caution: this should only be attempted on a high tide after a depth check by confident swimmers. Additionally, the harbour in St Andrews can be busy and swimmers should give priority to boats headed in and out.

As you paddle round the pier make sure you look back towards the iconic skyline of St Andrews. From this vantage, you can see St Rule's Tower, the cathedral ruins and the Gothic bell tower of St Salvator's Chapel rising into the sky.

From here, you can head directly along the coast into a small beach underneath the ruins of St Andrew's Castle, aptly named Castle Sands. There

are exposed rock formations along the edge of the cliff, so only competent paddlers should attempt this, as there is no exit option until you reach the beach. Despite having been abandoned for more than 400 years, the ruins still make for a dramatic view overhead as you paddle into the bay. The castle is now in the care of Historic Scotland, who have thankfully done much to preserve what is left of the structure.

Swimmers may wish to pause here and take a dip in the 'Castle Pool', an old tidal bathing pool that is still (mostly) standing. This beach and pool can also be accessed down a steep slope from The Scores, where there is pay-and-display roadside parking. Confident paddlers can continue from here, striking out from Castle Sands and turning left, heading towards West Sands, a beach famed for

its moment on the silver screen in *Chariots of Fire*. Once again, the coast is littered with exposed rocks, so a route slightly further out to sea should be taken to avoid them, particularly at high tide when some of the rocks may be concealed. Although this beach is more exposed to wind than East Sands, some shelter is offered by the dunes that separate it from the famous Old Course, the home of golf. West Sands also attracts a lot more swell than its neighbour East Sands, so if you can't find a wave to surf near the toastie shack do check out West Sands.

Although St Andrews isn't the most remote or dramatic adventure, it's incredibly special to spend time in a blue space closely surrounded by so much history. As urban adventures go, this is up there with the best.

GLASGOW
AND
SURROUNDS

THE RIVER CLYDE

Activities	Paddleboarding, kayaking
Experience level	✳ ✳ ✳
Environment	River
Start point	Riverside Museum car park
Carry time	Less than 5 mins
Public transport	Train or subway to Partick station
OS map	342

As I glided along the surface on my paddleboard and looked down into the murky depths of the River Clyde, I couldn't help but wonder at the stories this river would tell if it could.

It is said, 'Glasgow made the Clyde, and the Clyde made Glasgow'. This historic riverway has been key to the growth and success of the city since the first human settlements, from the tobacco and sugar trade in the 1700s to the rapid increase in shipbuilding in the 1800s and 1900s, and the river's pivotal role in the First and Second World Wars.

Modern-day investment in the city centre gives a new lease of life to this stretch of water, with business, residential and recreational buildings sprouting up along the riverside. For hundreds of years this river has witnessed ambition, success, failure and war as the city of Glasgow grew from its banks.

Rachel, Tegan and I met early one April morning, a touch before sunrise, in the car park of the Riverside Museum. The usual arduous task of pumping up the paddleboards was welcome as a

warm-up for our bodies as the cold Glaswegian air hovered around 0°C. To the right of the Riverside Museum, where the River Kelvin meets the Clyde, there is a short slipway into the water. We launched from here and turned immediately left onto the Clyde and paddled upriver towards some of Glasgow's most iconic modern-day landmarks.

Immediately you are greeted by the presence of the Tall Ship *Glenlee*. This restored Victorian sailing ship took to the high seas for almost 70 years before eventually returning to the Clyde. It is now a museum, showcasing its history. As we paddled past the hull of the ship, we saw our first Clyde seal bobbing up to take a good look at us. I am sure she was wondering what on earth we were doing up that early! This curious creature joined our watery city sightseeing tour and followed us upriver towards the unfolding Glasgow skyline.

On the right-hand side of the river, we glided past our second iconic ship of the morning, the paddle steamer *Waverley*. The ship's maiden voyage was in 1947, and after several fundraising campaigns

and a rebuild in early 2000 this passenger vessel is the last seagoing paddle steamer left in the world.

On the left-hand banks of the river stands the eye-catching SEC Armadillo, affectionately named due to its similarity to the four-legged armoured creature. Behind the Armadillo stands the OVO Hydro arena, where some of the world's most famous music artists come to perform in Glasgow. Catching your eye, a little further upriver is the historic Finnieston Crane, no longer operational but now an important symbol of the city's engineering past.

We continued our journey along the River Clyde, passing under the Clyde Arc, also known as the Squinty Bridge, then further upriver to its counterpart, the Tradeston Bridge, affectionately known as the squiggly bridge, before turning our boards around and retracing our paddle strokes back towards the Riverside Museum.

A sightseeing journey around Glasgow by paddleboard is an incredible way to experience the city and some of its key landmarks from a perspective usually reserved for the Clyde seals!

CANALS OF THE CENTRAL BELT

Activities	Paddleboarding, kayaking
Experience level	✽
Environment	Canal
Start point	Various locations
Carry time	Varies, usually very short
Public transport	Many bus and train transport links
OS map	342, 349 & 350

A snaking line of blue space weaves its way across Scotland's Central Belt, connecting its two largest cities, Glasgow and Edinburgh. In 2014, the Glasgow to Edinburgh Canoe Trail was formed, or as you may know it the Forth & Clyde and Union Canals. This trail extends for 54 miles through cities, towns and open countryside, providing many safe and accessible paddling opportunities for paddleboarders, kayakers and canoeists along its route.

Attempting this challenge in one go is a huge undertaking, but one enjoyed by hundreds of people each year. You can paddle the route in either direction, but it is generally easier to paddle west to east, from Glasgow to Edinburgh, with the prevailing wind on your back. The route begins on the Forth & Clyde Canal next to Pinkston watersports centre before heading out of Glasgow towards the town of Twechar, then on to the famous Falkirk Wheel, through the West Lothian towns of Linlithgow and Broxburn, and finally arriving in Edinburgh's city centre.

Any individual or groups planning to take on the Glasgow to Edinburgh Canoe Trail are asked to register their attempt on the Scottish Canals website. Here you will also find loads of information to help you plan a journey, including downloadable maps, key safety information and a list of local activity providers who can help with shuttle services and equipment hire.

Fortunately, this canoe trail does not need to be undertaken in one mighty expedition. There are countless points to launch from and too many brilliant routes for me to include in this book. I have had many great post-work paddles along this stretch of canal, from city centre exploration to finding calm and peace in the beautiful and often overlooked countryside of the Central Belt.

The Falkirk Wheel is a draw for many paddlers. The world's first and only rotating boat lift, it sits close to the halfway point of the Glasgow to Edinburgh Canoe Trail and its engineering prowess attracts many visitors each year. Opened by the Queen in 2002, this masterpiece connects the Forth & Clyde Canal with the Union Canal, uniting the cities of Glasgow and Edinburgh.

Rotating gondolas holding 500,000 litres of water transport the boats from the Forth & Clyde Canal at the bottom of the wheel to the Union Canal at the top, a lift of 35 vertical metres. Interestingly, the wheel only uses 1.5 kWh of energy to turn: this is the same amount as it would take to boil eight household kettles. There is even an annual challenge held at the wheel to see how many paddlers can fit and rotate on the Falkirk Wheel at the same time – something that sounds terrifying but I am sure is a lot of fun!

There are many paddling opportunities around the Falkirk Wheel. At this location you have your choice of canals: head east along the Union Canal towards Edinburgh, or west along the Forth & Clyde Canal to Glasgow, finding space to practise your paddling technique on the calm water.

The canals of the Central Belt offer super-accessible routes for all abilities and a brilliant way to access some blue space close to Scotland's most populated areas.

THE KELPIES

Activities	Paddleboarding, kayaking
Experience level	✱
Environment	Canal
Start point	The Kelpies car park
Carry time	5 minutes
Public transport	Bus connections from Falkirk
OS map	349

Named after the mystical Scottish legend of the shape-shifting aquatic horse, the kelpies towering above the Forth & Clyde Canal are very real and almost as notorious and fascinating as the legend itself.

The Kelpies stands 30 metres high, sculpted from metal into intricate horse-head structures, drawing your attention from miles around. They are known to many as a waymarker observed whilst driving up the M9 motorway. Thought to be designed to honour the working horses of Scotland,

who would have worked the land and pulled barges through Scotland's canal system, the sculpture is situated in Helix Park at the eastern entrance to the Forth & Clyde Canal.

Start your journey within Helix Park itself. Here you will find two car parks – the smaller one is only a slightly longer walk from The Kelpies and the second is larger (charges apply) and much closer to the sculptures themselves. At the heart of Helix Park is a visitor centre, fitted with a modern cafe and gift shop, enjoying stunning views over The Kelpies.

The paddle at The Kelpies is relatively straightforward. Jump on the canal close to the large car park and paddle down towards the backs of The Kelpies past reeds, pontoons, multicoloured canal boats and onlooking tourists. The paddle itself is nothing to write home about, but the opportunity to paddle close to one of Scotland's modern-day landmarks is very cool! Additionally, the lack of flowing water and tides make this an easier paddle than most, although the number of spectators certainly adds to the pressure not to fall in.

One of the best times to paddle here is after dark, when The Kelpies put on a light show and are illuminated by every colour of the rainbow. It can get pretty dark, so don't forget your head torch and be aware that the main car park is locked at 10 p.m.!

Falkirk-based paddleboarding company Paddlefast often runs socials to The Kelpies as part of their SUP club. You can head along to join them for an evening, or even rent or demo paddleboards from them.

The Kelpies might be one of the least 'adventurous' paddles in this book, but it is a very cool experience and they offer a great photo opportunity – pictures in front of these epic Scottish sculptures look awesome.

LOCH LOMOND

Activities	Paddleboarding, kayaking, swimming
Experience level	✱ ✱ ✱
Environment	Freshwater loch
Start point	Portnellan Farm
Carry time	Lochside parking
Public transport	Arrochar and Tarbet train station
OS map	OL 38 & 39

Loch Lomond lies just 25 miles north of Glasgow and is by far one of Scotland's most popular blue spaces. This loch is famous for good reason – it has it all. With a towering mountainous backdrop, including the ever-popular Ben Lomond, the loch's waters contain 22 islands and 27 smaller islets scattered across its surface. It has National Park status, as it forms a large part of the Loch Lomond & the Trossachs National Park, and you will find countless launch points along its shores for paddleboards and kayaks, with entry points for wild swimming too.

Loch Lomond is a monster of a loch: its waters stretch for 20 miles from the River Falloch in the north to the River Leven in the south, and it is up to 5 miles at its widest point. In fact, Loch Lomond is so large that it holds the record of being the largest lake by surface area in Great Britain and the second largest by volume after the mighty Loch Ness. You

could spend a lifetime exploring Loch Lomond and its expansive blue space, intricate shoreline and many secluded islands. It is worth noting that on Loch Lomond there are bylaws in place that state that paddleboarders and kayakers must always wear a life jacket or personal floatation device when on the loch.

One of our favourite spots from which to launch the paddleboards or kayaks is on the southern shore of Loch Lomond, where you will find Portnellan Organic Farm. There is a jetty extending down into the water next to a small beach for easy launching, and the farm itself has equipment for you to rent.

Once on the water, there is a magnitude of different routes to explore. You could head east or west to follow the stunning shoreline and visit the multiple small islets dotted around. We had our hearts set on the island of Inchmurrin, Loch Lomond's largest island, covering an area of 113

hectares. It has a permanent population of eight people, and even its own pub!

On the day we arrived at Portnellan it was a little too windy to make the crossing to Inchmurrin by paddleboard, so we opted to hire some sit-on-top kayaks from the farm and soon were floating towards the island. The weather conditions on Scotland's large lochs are often incredibly changeable, so it is always good to have adaptable adventure plans. Being able to hire kayaks was perfect for us on this day. From the shore, we headed for the most northerly point first, where two sandy beaches sit back-to-back. It takes around 30 minutes to reach this point by kayak, depending on the wind speed and direction. After a quick coffee and exploration of the beach, we paddled around the back of the island. The clouds were hugging the Munros surrounding the loch, so unfortunately it wasn't a day to get those spectacular views of Ben Lomond.

We circumnavigated the island and ended up at the Inchmurrin restaurant on the island's southern

tip, where we enjoyed a hearty pub lunch.

Our route in total was just over 5 miles and was a big undertaking, made easier by the stunning beaches and welcome pub en route.

At the far northern end of Loch Lomond the shores narrow, creating a very different experience to that at the southern end. A great spot to launch from in the north is Ardlui, close to where the River Falloch feeds into the main body of the loch. You can launch easily from the marina – just be cautious of speedboats and wake boarders also using this stretch of water.

In contrast to the quieter north shores, Loch Lomond's honeypot location is Luss. During the summer months, this place is busy with tourists and locals alike, soaking up this blue space. But again, it is all for good reason: Luss is stunning. Our advice is to head here on a quieter weekday or out of season to paddle out and explore the bulk of Loch Lomond's wonderful islands.

Loch Lomond is a stunning and accessible place to escape the city and soak up some blue health.

LOCH LONG

Activities	Swimming, paddleboarding, kayaking
Experience level	✱ ✱
Environment	Sea loch
Start point	Arrochar village hall
Carry time	N/A
Public transport	Direct bus connection from Glasgow
OS map	39

Nestled on the western edge of Loch Lomond & the Trossachs National Park is Loch Long, an extensive sea loch that begins in the Highland village of Arrochar and continues for 20 miles to reach the Firth of Clyde on Scotland's west coast. Loch Long has an interesting human history, an abundance of wildlife and there are plenty of options for exploring this blue space on and off the water.

Just 35 miles north of Glasgow, it is very accessible, with plenty of great facilities nearby, including a plethora of hotels, campsites, pubs, cafes and car parking. Due to its proximity to the watersports mecca of Loch Lomond, Loch Long can often be overlooked, but it is a hidden gem with so much opportunity for small and large adventures away from the crowds.

Unlike its neighbour, Loch Long is a sea loch and any adventure here is at the mercy of the tides. If you are aiming to swim or take a paddleboard or kayak journey here, aim for slack water around high tide when the loch will be at its fullest, with the least movement in the tidal system.

As a location for a long-distance paddleboard or kayak trip, Loch Long is incredible. However, in your planning do look at the restricted water zones around Coulport MOD base on the eastern banks.

A storage and loading facility for the UK's Trident Nuclear programme, it understandably has very strict security on the water surrounding it. If you are planning a paddle of the whole loch, study the nautical charts and keep to the western banks.

One of our favourite spots, far from even a thought of nuclear weapons, is the village of Arrochar on the northern tip of the loch, home to *Blue Scotland* photographer Rachel Keenan. The stunning Arrochar Alps rise from the opposite shore and the iconic craggy summit of the Cobbler commands the skyline, alongside its neighbour, the Munro Beinn Narnian.

On the day we visited, Rachel's partner Owen took the plunge into the loch's clear waters. We parked at Arrochar village hall, where there is a reasonably sized car park and a box for parking donations. In the water opposite the village hall are the remains of Arrochar Pier, built in 1850 to bring tourists by steamboat to Loch Long. Just up the road there are steps down to the water's edge and an easy sloping descent into the water. This launch site would also be a great way to enter the water via paddleboard or kayak and explore this end of Loch Long as an alternative to the two busier car parks at its northern end. After our swim, we headed to Cù Mara Bistro, just next door to the village hall – the perfect place to warm up with a coffee after an invigorating swim!

LOCH ARD

Activities	Paddleboarding, kayaking, swimming
Experience level	✴ ✴
Environment	Freshwater loch
Start point	Layby on east shore
Carry time	Less than 5 minutes
Public transport	N/A
OS map	OL 46

Picturesque Loch Ard, in Loch Lomond & the Trossachs National Park, is a must-visit blue space for swimming, kayaking and paddleboarding. Nestled amongst the Great Loch Ard Forest, its trees extend down to the water's edge and along its whole shoreline. At just 2.5 miles by 1 mile, this wee loch may be small, but it has huge potential for water-based adventures.

At Loch Ard, the seasons are reflected in the forest's canopy. We paddled here in early October just as the leaves were desperately holding on to the last of their chlorophyll. A matter of weeks later, the forest would give way to the full force of autumn and soon resemble a flaming fire, with oranges, yellows and reds erupting up from the edge of the loch. After the leaves have fallen in winter, you have the opportunity to see a snow-capped Ben Lomond looming over the far westerly end of the loch, and in spring and summer a luscious thick canopy engulfs the shoreline, alive with wildlife.

We joined friends Charlotte and Steve for an early morning exploration of Loch Ard by

paddleboard. They run The Adventure Photographers nearby and know this loch like the back of their hands.

We parked up at the eastern end of the loch, where there is a large layby on the B829, with space for around six cars. Just across the road you will find a shingle beach over a small wall to launch from. In the early morning light, the glassy water mirrored the jagged treeline of the forest. It almost seemed a shame to disturb this fragile picture with our paddle strokes, but the water was too inviting to resist.

We first explored the east side of the loch, heading through a small opening in the trees. At first glance it looked as though our route was no more than a stream. These are 'The Narrows', where the shores of Loch Ard taper in and the water gets fin-snappingly shallow. This is until the loch once again expands into a glorious large pool backed by quaint

boat houses and beautiful lochside homes. Loch Ard is often thought of as the source of the River Forth; if you were to continue east along these tributaries, you would soon be paddling down the River Forth and eventually meeting the salty water of the east coast near Edinburgh, some 30 miles later. A few years ago, Charlotte, Steve and Charlotte's mum, Clare, paddled the length of the River Forth from its source here at Loch Ard out to the sea in the Firth of Forth – it sounds like an excellent adventure, one for another book, perhaps?

We retraced our paddle strokes back to the main body of Loch Ard and went in search of Rob Roy's cave. Rob Roy was a Scottish outlaw who later became a folk hero. He is often described as the Scottish Robin Hood. Rob Roy's cave is on the southern shore of Loch Ard – it is marked on the OS map. Roy is thought to have hidden in the cave

whilst conducting raids or hiding from the Duke of Montrose's men. We tethered our boards to a tree below the spot where the cave is located and scrambled up a few metres of moss-covered rock until we found its dark opening. Crawling inside, there was only enough room for one person to lie flat alongside the spiders. We quickly left, as we spotted more and more of them emerging and were grateful not to have to follow in Rob Roy's footsteps, hiding out here from angry soldiers.

Loch Ard is home to several islands, the largest being Eilean Gorm at the loch's westerly end. To reach this island, people will often park at Kinlochard and launch from the small jetty there. We opted to explore the loch's southern edge, where there is a scattering of small islands and rocky outcrops a stone's throw from the shore. Located on one of the small islands is the ruin of Duke Murdoch's Castle,

also known as Dundochill Castle. At one point this small castle would have stood at a considerable height above the island, but a great fall in the early twentieth century reduced its prominence. Today the walls of the castle are almost intertwined with the island, as plants and trees grow from the ruins – you would be forgiven for not immediately spotting what is castle and what is island. We enjoyed a great hour jumping into the water and swimming in the peaty (and surprisingly warm) waters of Loch Ard until it was finally time to paddle back across the loch to our start point on the eastern shore.

Loch Ard's beautiful forest, mountainous backdrop and intricate shoreline make it a brilliant place to escape to in every season. Here you will find a wealth of adventure possibilities. Study your OS map and plot out your own adventure!

LAKE OF MENTEITH

Activities	Paddleboarding, kayaking, swimming
Experience level	✴
Environment	Lake
Start point	Car parks on north-east banks
Carry time	5 minutes
Public transport	Bus connections from Aberfoyle
OS map	OL 46

Lake of Menteith is low-lying, nestled in the rolling hills of Loch Lomond & the Trossachs National Park, 4 miles east of the quaint town of Aberfoyle. This lake is home to three islands, a busy trout fishery and a whole host of Scottish history. Lake of Menteith is relatively sheltered and reasonably shallow, with very easy access, making it a great beginner-friendly paddleboarding and wild swimming destination.

The name 'Lake' of Menteith is not a typo; it is, in fact, Scotland's only lake, as opposed to the countless lochs scattered across the country. In 1838, the UK Government's Ordnance Survey mapped the area for the first time, giving it its name, but before then this body of water was known as the 'Loch of Menteith'. There are many theories for this name change, but I haven't found much evidence to support any of them, so we will

accept this unusual body of water as Scotland's lone lake.

There are two good-sized car parks on the north-eastern banks of the lake; both are free and it's a very short walk across the minor road to the water's edge. You will find a scattering of small pebbly beaches from which to launch a paddleboard or swim. Lake of Menteith is a stocked trout fishery and on a warm weekend you will find dozens of small rental fishing boats buzzing around. It is also one of the main venues for the National Trout Fly Fishing Championships. When using the lake for recreation, give these small fishing boats a wide berth; only fly fishing is permitted from them and you don't want to be anywhere in their range.

There are three main islands in Lake of Menteith.

The smallest is Dog Isle and it sits close to the western shore of the lake. The second smallest is Inch Talla, where the ruins of the Earl of Meneith's castle remain. The largest island is Inchmahome, where an ancient priory lies, tucked away behind rare sweet chestnut trees. The priory was founded in 1238 as a quiet sanctuary for Augustinian canons. Throughout the centuries this island had many famous visitors, including Robert the Bruce in 1306 and Mary, Queen of Scots in 1547. Even today you can get a sense of the peace and tranquillity of this priory as you wander through its crumbling remains.

Lake of Menteith is a great beginner-friendly blue space for paddleboarding and wild swimming. It's close to the Central Belt, with interesting islands and history to explore.

LOCH AWE AND KILCHURN CASTLE

Activities	Paddleboarding, kayaking, swimming
Experience level	✳ ✳ ✳
Environment	Freshwater loch
Start point	Car park at Kilchurn Castle
Carry time	10 minutes +
Public transport	Bus links from Glasgow and Oban
OS map	360

Loch Awe is Scotland's longest freshwater loch, stretching for 25 watery miles through the western Highlands. Located just 20 miles from Oban, Loch Awe is often overlooked in the rush to reach Scotland's spectacular west coast. However, with its easy access from the main A85 road, ancient castles and islands to explore, and its stunning Highland backdrop, it is a brilliant blue space for paddleboarding, kayaking and swimming.

We opted to explore Loch Awe's north-eastern shores and the famed ruins of the fifteenth-century Kilchurn Castle. We parked up at the large castle car park, just off the A85. We had arrived late in the day and must have missed the main tourist rush, as the car park was almost deserted, giving us plenty of space to pump up the paddleboards. We followed the narrow path towards the castle until we spotted the Awe Viaduct, located just south of the confluence of the River Orchy and the River Strae. The viaduct is a beautifully constructed dark-green rail bridge spanning the river; in its shadows is a perfect pebbly point to launch from. Soon we were

gently paddling down the river, with the glorious Munro Ben Cruachan rising on our right-hand side. We didn't get our first glimpse of Kilchurn Castle until we had rounded the small headland and were in the main body of Loch Awe.

Kilchurn Castle sits at the head of Loch Awe in a commanding position over this vast waterway. The castle is one of the most photographed in Scotland, and it is easy to see why, with its five-storey tower house bestriding the ruin, and its barracks – the oldest surviving on the British mainland – and courtyard below. Kilchurn was the base of the Campbells of Glenorchy for over a century. During the medieval period this clan exercised great control over much of western Scotland. Today, the castle is free to visit and opens its doors between April and September.

Due to its sheer vastness, Loch Awe has a multitude of 'blue adventure' potential. Scattered throughout the loch are many islands to explore via kayak or paddleboard: some are just a stone's throw wide, while others are home to ruins of ancient castles and churches; another is inhabited to this day. About a mile south-west of the settlement of Lochawe, you will find Innis Chonain, a small, inhabited island, home to holiday accommodation. This is the easiest to access on Loch Awe, as it is connected to the mainland by a causeway.

Further south, you will find Innis Chonnel on Loch Awe's south-eastern shore. It's home to the ruin of the thirteenth-century Ardchonnel Castle, once a stronghold of the Campbell family. Directly opposite this small island is the settlement of Dalavich, where the pebbly beach stretching down to the shore is a great place to swim or from which to launch a paddleboard or kayak.

The vast Loch Awe offers a stunning location to paddle, swim or kayak, surrounded by jaw-dropping mountainous scenery. At 25 miles long, the loch itself has endless possibilities for swimming, paddleboarding and kayaking.

GREY MARE'S TAIL

Activities	Swimming
Experience level	★ ★ ★ ★
Environment	River & loch
Start point	Grey Mare's Tail car park, A708
Carry time	Under 1 hour
Public transport	N/A
OS map	330

Sometimes I find myself falling into the trap of always looking north for exciting adventures, enticed by the towering heights of Glen Coe or the dramatic shorelines of the North-east. However, the trip to visit Grey Mare's Tail cured me of this and was a wonderful reminder of how many magnificent blue spaces are situated in the Scottish Borders.

The walk up to the waterfall begins at the Grey Mare's Tail car park, which is managed by the National Trust for Scotland (NTS) and is pay-and-display. As we drove along the A708 to this spot, the view of the rolling hills of Moffat out of the window was making me very excited to get out and explore.

Historically there was a high path to the left of

the river (when looking towards the falls), however erosion has caused this to become unpassable, a fact that is not clear until you are some ways up the trail and reach a barrier erected by the NTS. Although this route does provide some nice views, it pales in comparison to the other path, and so I would recommend avoiding it.

The recommended alternative route involves crossing the river using a bridge and following a well-maintained path to the start of the trail. Here you will find several NTS information boards arranged in a circle amongst benches and small stone walls which point out landmarks on the trail, including White Coomb (a Corbett), and introduce the nearby nesting peregrine falcons.

From this point there are two possible blue spaces available to you. One of these is Loch Skeen, which, despite being 2.5 miles up the trail and 500 metres above sea level, is the easier to access. Follow a clear path that meanders beside the stream to the loch's edge. Keep your eyes peeled for a local herd of wild mountain goats which are reported to live in the area. Unfortunately I didn't see them on

my visit, but I'm assured they're there!

This loch is a stunning spot for a swim. Nestled into the Southern Uplands and framed by wild hills on each side, it truly feels remote. Due to its elevation, the water can get quite chilly, even in summer, so it's worth taking a hot drink with you, as there's a wee walk to get back to the car park and no facilities for several miles.

An alternative swimming spot is accessed from the same car park and by following the river up towards the waterfall along the bank. This route involves a bit of scrambling that, whilst not technically difficult, is made more challenging by the slippery conditions. I managed the trip very successfully with a 12-week-old puppy in my rucksack, but this should only be undertaken by competent scramblers who have appropriate footwear for the conditions.

We carefully made our way up the riverbank until we found a small rocky beach beside a gorge where the river narrows; here we made our base and headed into the water. At this point the current was flowing fairly slowly and we were able to scramble further upstream, finding pool upon pool of crisp, cold Scottish mountain water. Although this route does not have the same vast panorama as Loch Skeen, it's arguably more magical. The mossy crags of rock that frame the river on all sides and the sound of the waterfall in the distance only add to the atmosphere.

However, I will include a few words of caution: depending on the season, these damp conditions are the perfect breeding ground for Scotland's most hated pest – the midge! We did get some relief from them whilst in the water, as the constant flow of the river and waterfalls kept them moving. But whilst getting changed on the beach afterwards they were out in full force.

Additionally, this route should be approached with care. All of us on the trip (aside from the puppy) are experienced climbers who know our limits and what we're capable of. I would urge erring on the side of caution. Each of the pools is a stunning spot for a swim. We would recommend playing it safe, and if in doubt head up to the beautiful Loch Skeen for a swim right in the heart of the hills.

Grey Mare's Tail is a blue space found nestled in amongst mountains that feels quintessentially Scottish to me. This waterfall and loch combination really shows the best of what the Borders has to offer.

LOCH KEN

Activities	Paddleboarding, kayaking, swimming
Experience level	✷ ✷
Environment	Freshwater loch
Start point	Car park next to Loch Ken viaduct
Carry time	2 mins
Public transport	Bus connections from Dumfries
OS map	320

Sitting in the sparsely populated yet stunning Lowlands of Scotland, surrounded by countryside and forest, Loch Ken is a narrow but lengthy freshwater loch. It's fed by the Water of Ken at its northern end and extends for 9 miles through the glen to reach the River Dee at its southern tip. Loch Ken is a superb space in Dumfries and Galloway to paddleboard, kayak, swim and soak up rural blue health.

Loch Ken is located within what is known as the Galloway and Southern Ayrshire Biosphere. The area was awarded this accolade by UNESCO, recognising it as a world-class environment for nature and humans. This means that it is a brilliant place to live both for people and wildlife; it's chock full of incredible wild spaces on land and within its waterways. This quiet corner of Scotland is often overlooked, as people – myself included – look north

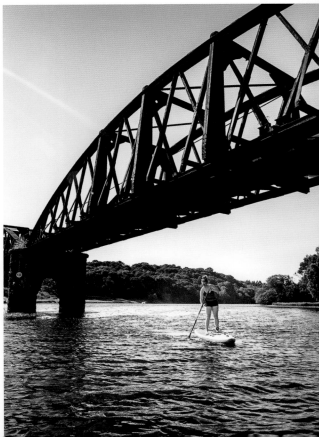

to the dramatic Highlands and coastlines for adventure, but Dumfries and Galloway, and Loch Ken in particular, is well worth a visit to experience blue space within the converted biosphere.

In terms of access to the loch, there are plenty of places along its length to get on the water. At its more northerly end is the Galloway Activity Centre, just off the A713. Here you will find a whole host of organised activities on and off the water, as well as accommodation. However, we were on the hunt for a quiet corner to experience a peaceful loch paddle and swim, so we headed further down the A713, past the Loch Ken marina until we reached a small car park next to the Loch Ken viaduct. Here we found a quaint stony beach leading into the water, and to our relief a shady area under the viaduct itself. The need to seek shade doesn't occur often in Scotland, but on this midsummer day the car thermometer was registering a sweltering 28°C – the shadows of the viaduct and the cool water of Loch Ken were a blessing indeed.

Whilst paddling or swimming in this area it is best to keep to the left side of the viaduct, just to avoid any boats coming in and out of the marina. We paddled south down the loch past the Loch Ken holiday park, a great-looking campsite that extends to the water's edge. Happy kids splashed about while parents sunbathed on the shore, faces smug with the realisation they had picked the best possible week of the year for a holiday. A couple of hundred metres from where the River Dee joins Loch Ken we found a haven of beautiful flowering lily pads. Here we relaxed in the sun, soaking up this awesome blue space.

Just before heading home, there was time for a quick swim under the old viaduct. This rusty-red structure has been towering over Loch Ken since 1861 and is the oldest standing bridge of its type in Scotland, closing in 1965 after more than a hundred years of service. When swimming under the bridge, do be aware of sunken debris and the hidden structure of the viaduct itself – we experienced a few bashed knees and toes here!

Loch Ken is a super-accessible loch, suitable for all ages and abilities to experience blue space set within a world-renowned ecosystem.

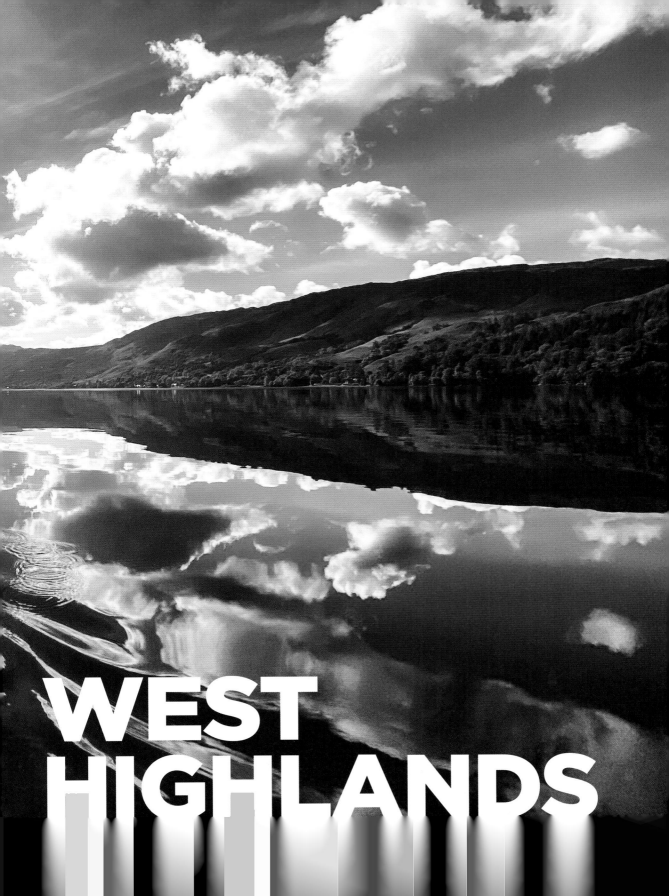

WEST
HIGHLANDS

LOCH MAREE

Activities	Paddleboarding, kayaking, swimming
Experience level	✦ ✦ ✦ ✦
Environment	Freshwater loch
Start point	Slattadale car park
Carry time	Lochside parking
Public transport	Bus service from Gairloch
OS map	433

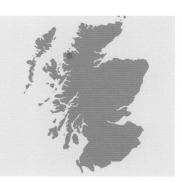

Located in the north-west Highlands, Loch Maree has captivated humans for centuries and has been a site of interest for many religions throughout the ages. This glacial trough is 110 metres deep and spans 12 miles from the Kinlochewe River in the south-east to the River Ewe in the north-west.

Loch Maree is home to 66 individual islands and, most fascinatingly, one of the islands has its own loch, with its own island. Loch Maree makes an incredible explorative paddleboard or kayaking destination, as well as a great place for a bracing swim.

The A832 runs along much of the southern shore of Loch Maree through what is known as the Beinn Eighe Nature Reserve, Britain's oldest nature reserve. This drive is simply stunning, especially when the

trees open and you can see the dotted islands of Loch Maree and its jaw-dropping mountainous backdrop. Along this stretch of road there are various options for lochside parking, with areas close by for launching crafts or from which to swim.

We chose to park at Slattadale. Here, you will find a tree-lined lochside car park with picnic tables, toilets, a beach and various walking routes from the car park itself. Looking out onto the loch, you can see a scattering of Loch Maree's islands littering the water's surface. Rising steeply from the opposite shore is Slioch, the imposing and mesmerising Munro that commands this waterway. Slioch is one

of the most photographed mountains in the Highlands and it is easy to see why. This huge, rocky outcrop draws your attention from miles around; it looks almost inaccessible from every angle, with its near vertical cliffs encircling the prized summit.

We got onto the water just as the early morning sun broke through the clouds and its rays illuminated the mountains on the opposite shore. We paddled straight for the nearest island, Eilean Ruairidh Mor, sitting just over half a mile from our launch point; it was a good warm-up for our adventure. From here we headed around the back of Garbh Eilean and were soon in a maze of islands, small rocky outcrops and dead-ended bays,

exploring this ancient landscape.

The islands of Loch Maree are the real draw to this blue space; they are steeped in unique fauna and flora, and incredible human history too. The larger islands of Loch Maree contain ancient Caledonian pine trees – some of the most pristine remnants of our ancient woodland left in Scotland, with some over 350 years old.

Loch Maree is also an incredibly important habitat for the black-throated diver, a beautiful migratory bird that feeds off these salmon- and trout-rich waters. In fact, 6 per cent of Britain's breeding pairs are located at Loch Maree.

In terms of the island's human history, this all centres around one of the loch's smallest islands, the aptly named Isle Maree. This wee island has been an important and well-documented religious site for Christians and Pagans for centuries, and interestingly there is also evidence of a prehistoric Iron Age circle, which has been dated back to 100 BC. On this small island you will also find the remains of a chapel, a graveyard, a holy well and a wishing tree. The wishing tree's fame originates with Queen Victoria's visit to Isle Maree in 1877. It has been said

that the Queen herself made an offering to the tree in the form of a coin wedged into its trunk. This exercise has been repeated by visitors ever since and now the old oak appears more metal than bark. Thank goodness it wasn't one of the protected ancient Caledonian pines!

We paddled back to Slattadale through a narrow channel separating Garbh Eilean and Eilean Sùbhainn. Caledonian pines extend down to the water's edge on each side and sharp, pointed mountains dress the horizon. This was the perfect way to end our paddle, only made better by a light tailwind gently guiding us to shore. Loch Maree had been on my paddling list for a long time and it totally lived up to my expectations. This is one location that I cannot wait to return to. During our morning paddle, we hardly scratched the surface of what this loch has to offer.

Loch Maree's sheer beauty and intricate web of islands have lured people to this blue space for hundreds, if not thousands, of years. It is a brilliant destination for an exploratory paddle, or something safe and easy next to the shore, or for a swim with a truly incredible backdrop.

EILEAN DONAN CASTLE AND THE THREE LOCHS

Activities	Paddleboarding, kayaking
Experience level	★ ★ ★
Environment	Sea lochs
Start point	Car park opposite Eilean Donan Castle
Carry time	Shore-side parking
Public transport	Bus services from Inverness
OS map	413

Eilean Donan Castle is located on a small tidal island in the western Highlands. This thirteenth-century castle is popular with tourists travelling across to the nearby Isle of Skye. Eilean Donan Castle has a long and fascinating history, but in modern times it has risen to fame after appearing in many films and TV shows, including James Bond and *Highlander*. In my opinion, there is no better way to experience one of Scotland's most famed and picturesque castles than from the water.

The castle sits at the meeting point of three sea lochs, Loch Duich, Loch Alsh and Loch Long. The ideal time to paddle here is in the slack water before high tide; as the tide drops, the water drains out towards the sea at speed, meaning that care, experience and accurate tide planning are needed.

There are various launch points to choose from when exploring the castle and surrounding lochs by kayak or paddleboard, including a large car park at the castle itself. However, this car park is often busy

with visitors and personally I don't much enjoy pumping up my paddleboard with an audience! Instead, we headed to the other side of the A87 bridge, beside Dornie Community Hall and opposite the spectacular castle. There is a smaller car park, cafe, public toilets and a handy slipway into the mouth of Loch Long.

Paddling directly towards the castle gives you a sense of the majesty of this ancient building; it is a very special way to experience some of Scotland's history. The island had been inhabited for some time before the first fortified structure was built here. It was seen as a key defensive position against Viking raiders who controlled much of northern Scotland at this time.

At high tide, you can paddle directly under the old stone bridge which connects Eilean Donan island to the mainland. Be warned – you may attract a lot of attention from the tourists visiting by foot above you. Not a good time to fall in!

After exploring the island, you can either head south-east and explore Loch Duich – the far side of the loch, away from the noisy A87, is recommended. Alternatively, you can point south-west and explore Loch Alsh, including some of its larger islands.

Whilst paddling, make sure to keep your eyes peeled for sea otters and seals, who are often spotted in this area. Whilst visiting, we had a particularly inquisitive seal follow us for some distance.

The history, the mesmerising backdrop of the Highlands and the Isle of Skye, and the ability to make the landlubbing castle visitors jealous makes this a truly epic paddle!

LOCH SHIEL AND GLENFINNAN

Activities	Paddleboarding, kayaking, swimming
Experience level	✶ ✶
Environment	Freshwater loch
Start point	Glenfinnan Visitor Centre
Carry time	10–15 mins
Public transport	Train to Glenfinnan
OS map	391 & 398

Loch Sheil is a stunning loch situated to the west of the Highland hub of Fort William. At 17 miles long, Loch Shiel is Scotland's fourth-longest loch and an epic place for a paddle. Surrounded by towering mountains on its famous north-eastern shore, this area is steeped in Scottish history, as well as being a modern-day attraction. This was where the Jacobite rising began in 1745, but in more recent times the Glenfinnan Viaduct features in the *Harry Potter* films – the *Hogwarts Express* makes the journey across the viaduct on its way to Hogwarts school. Despite all the fanfare on the shore, Loch Shiel is brilliant for a paddle, with an island to explore, mountains to be mesmerised by and a famous steam train to keep an eye out for.

There are various entry points to the loch, but after driving around and meeting a few dead ends and 'no parking' zones we left our vehicle at the Glenfinnan Visitor Centre. Here you will find toilets, a cafe and local area information, as well as a whole lot of tourists. On a summer's day, this car park is a busy place, but it is worth persevering; you will find peace and tranquillity when eventually you get out on the loch. From the car park, you must cross the busy A830 road; this can be tricky with a huge paddleboard or kayak, so do take care. From here, you can follow the flow of people down towards the Glenfinnan Monument and access the loch just behind it.

The Glenfinnan Monument was erected in 1815 as a tribute to the loyal Jacobites who rallied behind Bonnie Prince Charlie in his attempt to regain the British throne. On 19 August 1745, a ceremony took place at Glenfinnan to mark support from

Highland chiefs and clans for the claim that Charles's father was the true King of Britain, with Charles being the Prince Regent. The monument stands at 18 metres high and is a brilliant sight from on and off the loch.

Here you can launch onto the water via paddleboard or kayak and soon be away from the crowds to explore the shores of this famous blue space. If you are here to swim and don't fancy stripping off in front of tourists, cross the footbridge over the Callop River and follow a good path down the south-eastern shore until you find your perfect swim spot. There is a vast array of wildlife here, including some awesome bird life. Make sure to scan the skies, as golden eagles have been spotted in this area, along with white-tailed sea eagles and peregrine falcons. Loch Shiel is a Special Protected Area (SPA) due to the importance of these birds and as a breeding ground for the black-throated diver.

There is also an island not too far from the shore to paddle round. The island goes by the name of Eilean Ghleann Fhionainn – and even with my very bad grasp of Gaelic, I can make out what that one means! However, the best part of this paddle must be the towering mountains rising steeply from the loch's surface. They are totally enchanting and make it easy to forget the hustle and bustle of the shore.

Loch Shiel is beautiful. Nestled in the mountains of the Highlands, it is a brilliant place to paddle or swim. This area is famed all over the world – mainly for its significance in Scottish history, but more and more so because of its modern-day wizarding connections!

LOCH MOIDART AND CASTLE TIORAM

Activities	Paddleboarding, kayaking, swimming
Experience level	★ ★ ★ ★
Environment	Sea loch
Start point	Along the northern shore or at the castle
Carry time	Lochside parking
Public transport	Bus links from Fort William
OS map	390

Loch Moidart is a double-pronged sea loch in the western Highlands of Scotland. It is a haven for kayakers and paddlers; the loch boasts a medieval castle, several islands and two narrow channels to explore. Loch Moidart runs for almost 5 miles from the River Moidart in the east to the open ocean in the west.

There are a couple of options for accessing Loch Moidart. If you are interested in a short adventure or would like to paddleboard here, you can park reasonably close to one of the main attractions, Castle Tioram. You will find a small parking area at the end of a long, single-track road off the A861. When planning your trip, do bear in mind that Loch Moidart is a tidal sea loch, with the water draining out of this area twice a day. You will be able to paddle here an hour or so each side of high tide.

For our trip, we were aiming to explore the

whole of Loch Moidart, so we chose a launch point on its northern shore. The A861 runs along much of this shoreline and when coming from the west there is a large parking layby just before you reach The Old Mill. Here, there is enough space for three or four cars and a slipway hidden in the trees for launching onto the loch itself.

For our kayaking trip, we joined Andreas Heinzl, owner of sea-kayaking company Unexplored Scotland. Andreas runs adventurous kayaking tours along the west coast of Scotland, from Skye to Knoydart and along the glorious Arisaig coastline, so he knows this stretch of intricate sea lochs and open ocean like the back of his hand.

From our launch point, we crossed to the loch's southern shore and used it as a handrail until we got our first view of the medieval Castle Tioram. Sitting proudly on a small tidal island where the River Sheil flows into the main body of Loch Moidart, Castle Tioram was for centuries of great strategic importance at this junction of waterways. There is a short sandy causeway linking the mainland to the castle.

The castle is currently closed, so you cannot access the interior, however absorbing the beauty of this place from the beach or water is a rewarding experience and makes this trip worthwhile.

Loch Moidart has several islands to explore from the water, with the largest being Eilean Shona, a stunning tidal island. Eilean Shona splits Loch Moidart in two, creating a south channel and a north channel, both feeding out to the ocean. This gives you two options for paddling out to sea from Loch Moidart. The wide south channel is still navigable on a low tide, whereas the north channel drains out rapidly, leaving it impassable at low water. However, the north channel's narrow sides and stunning scenery make for a much more dramatic paddle.

We had our hearts set on exiting Loch Moidart by this north channel but may have spent a little too much time exploring Castle Tioram; the tide was quickly retreating by the time we eventually reached the head of the north channel. For a nerve-wracking few minutes we passed over the shallowest section of the channel with a foot or so of water to spare, carefully placing our paddles so as not to scrape them on the loch's floor. If we had waited another 30 minutes, we would not have made it out. As you paddle down the north channel, the views get better and better until you get your first glimpse of the Isle of Eigg on the horizon, framed by the steep sides of the valley. From the entrance to Loch Moidart, you can continue north or south along the coastline or wait for the tide to turn and retrace your paddle strokes back up to your launch point.

Loch Moidart is a remote sea loch with stunning vistas in every direction. A journey into this blue space gives you a real sense of ancient Scotland, with its historic castle, towering mountains and untouched islands. Tidal planning and careful execution are needed to make the most of this incredible area.

ARISAIG SKERRIES

Activities	Paddleboarding, kayaking
Experience level	★ ★ ★ ★ ★
Environment	Ocean
Start point	Arisaig village
Carry time	5–10 minutes, depending on the tide
Public transport	Arisaig train station
OS map	398

On a bright sunny day, the coastline around the small, quaint village of Arisaig can resemble the Caribbean. In fact, its clear, shallow waters, where you can peer down to the seabed, its glorious white sand, a wealth of wildlife and its mountainous backdrop of the Skye Cuillins and Rum, as well as the Isle of Eigg's imposing An Sgurr, make this corner of the world – in my (potentially controversial) opinion – far superior to any Caribbean island.

The Arisaig Skerries are a collection of small

islands and semi-submerged rocks that litter the entrance to Loch nan Ceall, at the head of which lies the village of Arisaig. Twice a day, every day, the interconnecting terrain of the Arisaig Skerries changes from ocean to land and back again. At high tide only the tallest points of the islands are visible, but as the tide pushes out, this landscape shifts to expose an extensive network of sandbars connecting many of these islands.

The Arisaig Skerries are a brilliant place to explore by kayak or paddleboard for experienced paddlers: the wealth of wildlife and adventure potential out there is incredible. If in doubt about your experience, I would highly recommend joining a guided trip to the skerries with one of the many local kayak and paddleboard schools.

There are various places in and around Arisaig to launch from, depending on the tide and type of adventure you are interested in. To the north of the village, there is a beautiful, sheltered bay near the campsite at Gortenachullish that makes a good launch point; from here, you will have to paddle around Eilean Ighe to get into the skerries. This paddle can feel a little exposed, but you are rewarded with breathtaking views of the mountainous Isle of Skye on the near horizon. Alternatively, you can launch from Arisaig village itself or the road that leads out of the village and follows much of the southern shore of Loch nan Ceall.

The Arisaig Skerries are made up of a north channel and a south channel. Both are exposed to reasonably fast tidal flow, wind and waves, but shelter can be found amongst the skerries themselves.

The Arisaig Skerries are renowned for their huge population of common seals drying off on the rocky

outcrops at low tide and hunting in the clear waters at high tide. Even though they are named the common seal, there is actually a larger population of grey seals than common in the waters of Scotland. The smaller common – or, as it is often known, harbour seal – is usually found on sheltered shores, in estuaries and on sandbanks, making the Arisaig Skerries the perfect home for these friendly dogs of the water. When viewing seals perched on their rocks, it is of utmost importance to keep your distance from them, at least 100 metres or more. Seals haul out of the water to rest and often to nurse their young; they also need this time to moult and replace fur, which is essential for their thermoregulation. If you get too close, the seal will get frightened and dive back into the water at speed, disturbing this important process and risking an injury by scrambling over sharp rocks. Let the swimming seals come to you. Here in the Arisaig Skerries, these beasts are inquisitive.

To help us explore the Arisaig Skerries, we took kayaking guide Andreas Heinzl, the owner of sea-kayaking company Unexplored Scotland. We pointed our kayaks south, down the coastline and around the Rhu Peninsula, our target for an evening camp being Rhu Point Beach, one of the finest wee beaches I have had the pleasure of camping beside in Scotland. It is a small stretch of white sand with the most incredibly clear water, and from the nearby hilltop you have panoramic views of the isles of Skye, Rum, Muck and Eigg.

Andreas cooked us an incredible spaghetti carbonara on his camp stove while we watched the sun set over the islands and sipped Scottish whisky, the perfect end to an amazing day on the west coast of Scotland.

The Arisaig Skerries are incredible to experience but should only be paddled to by experienced kayakers and paddleboarders. If in doubt, don't miss out: hire yourself a guide for the trip.

THE ARDNISH PENINSULA

Activities	Paddleboarding, kayaking
Experience level	★ ★ ★ ★
Environment	Sea loch
Start point	Layby at the Prince's Cairn
Carry time	5 minutes
Public transport	N/A
OS map	398

The wild and remote Ardnish Peninsula lies just south of the town of Arisaig on the rugged west coast of Scotland. Today, it is an uninhabited expanse, but its human past can still be felt on the land, with its abandoned crofting villages lining the shore and the remains of Viking longboat houses – and the one remaining building: the Peanmeanach Bothy.

On the water, there are a magnitude of places to explore via sea kayak and, in favourable weather, journeys by paddleboard for more experienced paddlers. From secluded white sandy coves to deserted islands and extensive sea lochs, this area is an incredible playground for those with a sense of adventure. There is no road access to the Ardnish Peninsula, which adds to the charm of adventures in this remote corner of Scotland. However, this means that time needs to be taken to study your map and choose whether to approach the peninsula from the loch to the north or the loch to the south.

Lapping on the northern shore of the Ardnish Peninsula is Loch nan Uamh, a wide sea loch opening up into the Sound of Arisaig. On the opposite shore to the peninsula there is a launch site just off the A830, marked on the map as the Prince's Cairn. Here you will find a large layby on the shore side of the road and, just a short walk away, a sizeable cairn and plaque marking the spot where Bonnie Prince Charlie departed for France following the failed Jacobite rising of 1745. This is a great option for launching your craft – maybe not for a journey to France, but for a paddle across to the remote and alluring Ardnish Peninsula. Depending on the conditions, and your interest, you can handrail the coastline or point straight across Loch nan Uamh.

Wrapping around the southern shore of the peninsula is a second sea loch, Loch Ailort. Dotted with rocky islands, some with their own sandy beaches and hidden coves, this narrow sea loch is a brilliant body of water to explore and has the potential for many multi-day adventures. We pinpointed Peanmeanach, the most well-known point on the peninsula, to be our wild camping destination.

Peanmeanach was once a thriving township, with a population of around 50 people. Today you will find only the tumbling remains of the stone crofts, but also the Peanmeanach Bothy, which has been restored over recent years. It is private, so you can't just pitch up, but you can visit the Ardnish website to book it out for the ultimate unplugged break in this stunning corner of the country.

We opted to stick with our tents and pitched up on the grassy outcrop just back from the beach, soon lighting our barbecue and opening the whisky. There aren't many better feelings than watching the sun dip below the horizon from a comfy camp after a long day on the water.

LOCH MORAR

Activities	Paddleboarding, kayaking, swimming
Experience level	✷ ✷
Environment	Freshwater loch
Start point	Along the northern shore
Carry time	Lochside parking
Public transport	Morar train station
OS map	398

Nestled in the mountains, close to the ever-popular Silver Sands beach, Loch Morar offers a stunning setting for a swim or a paddle around its many islands. Make sure to keep your wits about you when exploring Loch Morar, as it is the home of Morag, a rarely sighted (and potentially mythical) aquatic beast!

Loch Morar is a deep gash across the landscape, running almost perfectly from east to west. From the towering, remote mountains of Lochaber in the east to the River Morar in the west, here water flows from the loch a short but steep distance down to the white sands and clear waters of the Arisaig coastline. Loch Morar's second claim to fame – after Morag, that is – is the fact that it is the deepest freshwater body of water in the British Isles, with a maximum

depth of 310 metres – that's over 1,000 feet!

The far eastern end of the loch is incredibly remote and only accessible by foot. Maybe this fact, along with the sheer depth of the water, gives more plausibility to tales of a monster residing here than similar tales of its cousin on the busy waters of Loch Ness. It is said that whenever Morag was sighted she brought about the death of a member of the local McDonald clan. Luckily for us water users, and for the McDonald clan, the most common sightings here are of some special Scottish wildlife, including otters, red deer, golden eagles and even the illusive sea eagle.

The more accessible western end of Loch Morar is where we headed for our early morning paddle out to the islands. There is a road that runs along part of the northern shore and it offers a few good places to launch a paddleboard or kayak from, between the ornate church and the hamlet of Bracara, including a couple of small beaches and jetties.

We arrived soon after sunrise, with the aim of catching some early morning light, but unfortunately the reality differed from the forecast: thick clouds covered much of the sky. However, there was not a breath of wind on the loch, its surface mirroring the stunning scenery in every direction.

We slowly paddled out towards the islands, apprehensive to disturb this beautifully still surface with our paddle strokes.

Loch Morar has four main islands to explore and a handful of small rocky lumps jutting out of the water. Like all loch islands, we tend to avoid setting foot on them, especially during bird-nesting season. Luckily, the islands of Loch Morar are a joy to observe from the water. They have an almost prehistoric feel, clad in trees growing out of the rock at uncomfortable-looking angles and strange jagged rock formations protruding from the shallows.

No matter what point you launch from, the paddle out to the islands is a reasonable distance and would be a tough experience in windy conditions. So bear this in mind when assessing your abilities for this paddle.

Loch Morar is an awesome place for wild swimming, with great beaches and jetties along the northern shore as easy points of entry into the water.

Even with its proximity to the hubs of Arisaig and Malaig, Loch Morar has a remote and wild feel. The western end is a superb place for relaxed paddleboarding, kayaking and swimming, while the remote eastern end offers the potential for a much bigger adventure.

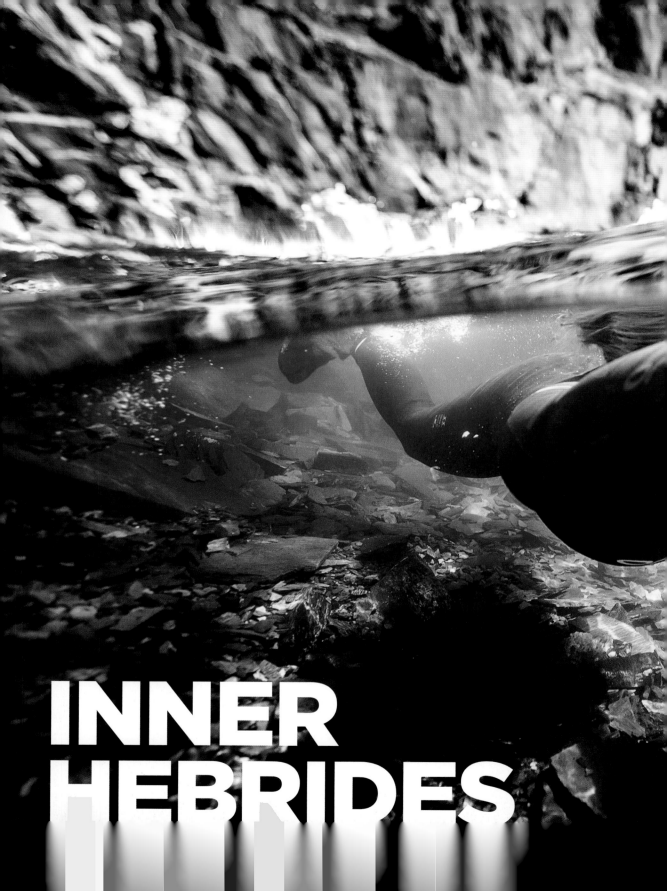

INNER
HEBRIDES

SLATE QUARRIES, EASDALE ISLAND

Activities	Swimming
Experience level	✱ ✱ ✱
Environment	Flooded quarry
Start point	Car park at Ellenabeich
Carry time	20-minute walk
Public transport	Bus connections from Oban
OS map	359

Easdale Island, tucked in the Firth of Lorn, 15 miles south of Oban, is a wild swimmer's dream. Here you can experience an otherworldly blue space in steep-sided slate quarries filled with incredible clear blue waters. There are multiple filled quarries dotted around this small island, all a stone's throw from the ocean. Speaking of stone throwing, each September Easdale Island hosts the world stone-skimming championship, where competitors from across the globe compete to see who can skim a slate stone the furthest distance at these incredible pools.

The Easdale Island adventure begins with the

outward journey. To reach this magical island, take the B844 off the main Oban road. Soon you will cross the famous Clachan Bridge, an eighteenth-century hump-backed bridge connecting the island of Seil to mainland Scotland. After weaving your way across this quaint island, you will reach its main village, Ellenabeich, where you will find a large car park by the harbour where you can leave the car for the day; if you are travelling by bus from Oban, it will drop you here. From the harbour, you have fantastic views of Easdale Island and the craggy outcrops of its slate quarries.

Easdale is car-free, so unless you are planning to kayak or paddleboard across, the only way to reach it is by the small passenger ferry from the harbour. The journey takes little more than five minutes each way. You will be greeted by rows of charming white cottages, with piles of slate wherever you look – and wheelbarrows, used by locals for transporting their shopping home. There is a maze of paths leading all over the island, so pick your route carefully so as to not end up in someone's back garden (like we did!). The slate quarries for swimming can be found on the far west side.

When commercial slate quarrying ended here, the population dramatically fell over the following decades. However, the population is on the rise again and currently there are around 60 permanent residents. As you walk across this quiet island you get a real sense of community here; it is easy to see why this blissful life could be attractive.

Easdale sits within a group of islands off Scotland's west coast known as the Slate Islands, affectionately thought of as the 'islands that roofed the world'. For centuries they were at the centre of the slate-quarrying industry and have roofed many notable buildings across Scotland, including Glasgow Cathedral and Castle Stalker. At the height of the industry the working population of Easdale would have been close to 500, operating up to seven quarries at one time. In 1881, there was a huge blow to the industry when a massive storm hit the island, with towering waves filling many of the quarries. Without the modern means to pump out this sea water, quarrying slowed rapidly, until the last commercial stone was cut in the 1950s.

On the west side of the island, the L-shaped quarry is often the most popular for swimming. This pool is shallower than the others, meaning the water might be a little warmer. It is also often protected from the prevailing winds. From here, you have fantastic views out over the isle of Mull, as well as Scarba and many small skerries. However, on the day that Rachel and I visited Easdale a chilly easterly wind was blowing straight across the pool and the idea of entering the water here suddenly became very unappealing. We re-traced our steps back to the first pool we had walked past – this one was surrounded by steep cliffs on each side and was much more protected from the wind.

Our swim began tentatively. There were no other swimmers there and barely a soul in sight on the island. The sides drop away sharply into the quarry, so there is no easing in. I would really recommend wearing a wetsuit and having a float, especially if it is your first time at Easdale – the waters of the slate quarries are icy cold; cold-water shock could quickly affect you with this sudden immersion. The temperature is partly due to their sheer depth: I have seen reports that these pools go down to between 60 and 90 metres. Now, that is deep! Can you imagine almost two Olympic swimming pools below you as you swim? For Rachel and me, there was something quite eerie about being in water this deep, especially with no one else around, and thinking about the fact that it was an abandoned quarry.

After just five minutes in the water, the sun had burnt through the cloud and began to illuminate this clear water, transforming it into a turquoise oasis. The sun also seemed to pull away the slightly eerie feel of this island, and we quickly relaxed and reverted to being hyper kids at a swimming pool. We jumped from the rocks into the deep water, dove as deep as we could and explored this underwater world with our goggles on. Time quickly flew by and before we knew it we had been playing in the quarries' icy waters for over an hour. As we walked back to catch our ferry, we spotted the Puffin restaurant and bar next to the harbour, the perfect place to warm up after a chilly swim.

Easdale Island is by far one of the coolest places we have swum in Scotland. The whole journey is part of the adventure, and this is a day we highly recommend.

FIDDEN BEACH, MULL

Activities	Swimming, paddleboarding, kayaking
Experience level	*
Environment	Ocean
Start point	Designated parking area near Fidden Farm
Carry time	5–10 mins depending on the tide
Public transport	Calmac ferry from Oban
OS map	373

We visited the beach at Fidden Farm on a mid-winter trip to Mull, weaving our way through snow-capped hills and stunning views of the island to reach this spot. Although it was quiet when we visited (our only company being some curious sheep), if you're planning on making the trip during the summer months be aware this area can become slightly busier due to the presence of a campsite there. Additionally, Fidden is a fully working farm, with livestock, and care should be taken to ensure that you park in the designated

areas and keep dogs under close control.

Unlike the vast expanses of golden sand that you see in the Outer Hebrides, Fidden is characterised by the craggy rocks that jut out along the beach, getting larger and more frequent all the way to the island of Iona on the horizon. This rugged addition adds character to a landscape that is complemented by lovely sand and the crystal-clear water that makes so many of these Hebridean swim spots so impressive.

We planned on a sunset wild swim at Fidden

and, thanks to the shorter days, the weak winter sun was just starting to set as we made our way across the beach to the water mid-afternoon. We were visiting Mull in the aftermath of one of the worst storms of the winter and the gentle calm of the water and the peacefulness of the beach was a welcome reprieve from the wild weather we had experienced the day before.

This beach is a real gem for wild swimmers. We'd particularly recommend it to those who are new to wild or ocean swimming – many of the spots were protected by the large rocks, which makes for a serene swim, plus the long expanse of flat beach means that you can swim for a reasonable distance without being out of your depth.

Since our trip to Mull, lots of folks have reached out to tell us that Fidden is a spot that is special to them, that holds memories of family trips, camping and long summer days on the beach. It's easy to see why it sticks in the mind. The easy access makes this beach accessible to most, with the reward of crystal-clear water and a stunning view out to Iona.

EAS FORS WATERFALL, MULL

Activities	Swimming
Experience level	* *
Environment	River
Start point	Parking area next to B8073
Carry time	Less than 5 mins
Public transport	Calmac ferry from Oban
OS map	372

Eas Fors is one of the most stunning waterfalls on Mull. It's the perfect place for an icy dunk while soaking up the expansive sea views of this Inner Hebridean gem.

The falls here come in a set of three. The upper falls are located above the road and possess no great interest for wild swimmers. The lower falls drop precariously off a cliff, falling 30 metres to amalgamate with the salty water below (caution needs to be taken here, especially if you are planning on bringing small children or dogs). However, at the middle falls you will find a grassy area, perfect for a picnic, a deep freshwater pool and a cascading waterfall, topping up the swimming pool around the clock with icy water.

Interestingly, the name comes in a set of three, too: Eas Fors Waterfall is translated as the word 'waterfall' three times – *Eas* is Gaelic for waterfall; Fors is Norse for waterfall, and we all know the English!

This destination is reasonably easy to reach. It is located just off the coast road around Loch Tuath. If travelling from the south, the falls can be found a couple of miles north of the Ulva ferry link. As you travel along this single-track road, hugging the coastline, you will come across a small, unmarked parking area on the right-hand side, just before the bridge, where you will find enough parking for six or seven cars. The falls themselves are just a short walk away: head up the road towards the river and before the bridge you will spot a small track on your left-hand side. Follow the track as it heads steeply downhill to a grassy clearing next to the waterfall.

We visited Eas Fors during winter. The snow-clad mountains of the island had undergone an overnight thaw and meltwater flowed from the high points of the island through the river systems and eventually into the lochs and the ocean. At Eas Fors, the water energetically cascading down was icy to touch, but the sun was shining and the blue sky above illuminated the pool, creating an alluring swimming prospect. Clad in 5 mm neoprene suits and boots, we entered this turbulent pool for a brisk but thoroughly energising swim – promising ourselves to one day return on a warm summer's day!

Eas Fors Waterfall is an easy-to-access mini adventure on the Isle of Mull. A dip into the icy water of the middle falls is an incredibly rewarding endeavour, but the blue health benefits of this spectacle can also be absorbed from the warmth of the grassy banks surrounding the pool.

CALGARY BAY, MULL

Activities	Swimming, paddleboarding, kayaking
Experience level	*
Environment	Ocean
Start point	Car park at both north and south ends of the beach
Carry time	5 mins from north side car park
Public transport	Calmac ferry from Oban
OS map	374

Calgary Bay is a cracking bit of blue health tucked away on the north-western coast of Mull. It's hugged on both sides by looming hills that extend away into the ocean, creating the bay. The bright, white sand blends seamlessly into the surrounding machair that is synonymous with beaches in the Hebrides. Due to the vulnerability of this grass, it's particularly important to leave no trace, which includes only parking in designated areas and not lighting fires.

Your trip to the beach can start in one of two locations, each with their own merit. On the north side is a larger car park that is host to an unusual-looking ice-cream hut made from bits of salvaged boats and other flotsam and jetsam. At the other edge of the beach is a second, much smaller car park that sadly does not have ice-cream but does have public toilets. All the facilities in the area are maintained by volunteers from the local Friends of Calgary Bay group.

This bay is one of the largest and most popular

on Mull and really is awe-inspiring. It's a great spot for a family trip, as there is something for everyone. It is easily accessible, has lots of wide, open space and also has some great rockpools – we passed some time coming through them looking for anemones, crabs and other wildlife.

While Calgary Bay is a great spot for wild swimming since the water is as clear as we have come to expect from the Hebrides, it truly calls out to paddleboarders and kayakers. There's so much to explore from the perspective of the board, with great views on all sides, including back towards land. We spent an incredible morning here, soaking up the winter sunshine and having a relaxed paddle around the bay. Just as we were packing up at the car, we spotted a pod of dolphins playfully jumping out of the water. An incredible way to end our session.

This is an awesome spot to take in some of the benefits of blue health. It's a very accessible beach, which rewards you with its wide, open space. It's well worth the trip to spend some time appreciating this quintessential Hebridean beach.

IONA

Activities	Swimming, paddleboarding, kayaking
Experience level	✻ ✻
Environment	Ocean
Start point	Ferry pier on Iona
Carry time	5–30 mins
Public transport	Calmac ferry from Mull
OS map	373

Nestled 1 mile off the west coast of Mull is the crown jewel of the Inner Hebrides: Iona. A miniature island at just 1.5 miles wide by 3 miles long, what this island lacks in mileage it makes up for in tranquil beauty.

Iona is often thought of as the cradle of Scottish Christianity. In AD 563 St Columba landed on her sandy shores from Ireland, using Iona as a launch point as he pushed into mainland Scotland, converting many of previously Pagan faith to Christianity. To this day, Iona remains a place of pilgrimage for those of faith and those seeking the tranquillity of this stunning blue space.

When planning a trip to Iona, the first thing to be aware of is that this is a car-free island for visitors. In 1978, an order was created to limit the number of vehicles to preserve this incredible habitat. You can leave your car next to the terminal at Fionnphort on Mull before making the crossing by Calmac ferry. As

a visitor, this order is a blessing. The island remains a quiet and tranquil space, easily traversed by foot. For those laden with luggage or less able, there is an island taxi service and often accommodation providers will run shuttles from the ferry terminal. This may require a little more planning for those blue-space enthusiasts wanting to bring across large paddleboards or kayaks; it is partly for that reason we have only ever used Iona as a wild swimming destination and, my goodness, what an epic wild swimming destination it is!

There are brilliant beaches on every coast of Iona, all with glorious white sand and turquoise-tinted waters. On the sprawling west coast of the island is a long stretch of white sandy beaches known as the Bay at the Back of the Ocean, reached by Iona's only east–to–west road. This is a beautiful bay to visit, but it has been known for strong tides, so do enter the water with caution. Better yet, save your swim for a beach five minutes' walk to the north – the glorious bay of Port Ban, one of the Inner Hebrides' premier wild swimming locations.

Port Ban beach is flanked on both sides by large rocky outcrops, creating a sheltered, shallow bay that even feels a wee bit warmer than other spots on the island. This is a brilliant and reasonably safe beginner- and family-friendly swimming spot; you will find crystal-clear water down to the sandy sea floor and colourful kelp beds occupying part of the bay. The sand here is more broken shells than fine sand, but give it another 500 years and it will resemble the Caribbean! Swimming shoes or wetsuit boots are useful here, and don't forget your mask and snorkel for the kelp beds. If you choose to head here straight from the ferry, it is just a 20-minute walk due west of the pier.

Looking to the north of Iona, the island quickly narrows to a point, with glorious beaches on both the east and west sides. On the west side you will find one of our favourite spots, a mesmerising beach known as Calbha, always quieter than other places on Iona. There is brilliant swimming here, with the backdrop of the alluring Calbha island.

Iona has everything you need to detox from modern life and reset: incredible scenery, quiet and tranquil island vibes, and inviting clear blue waters.

TIREE

Activities	Paddleboarding, surfing, kayaking, swimming
Experience level	✳ ✳ ✳
Environment	Ocean
Start point	Various locations
Carry time	Usually not far at all
Public transport	Calmac ferry from Oban
OS map	372

Tiree is the most westerly isle of the Inner Hebrides and is Scotland's mecca for watersports. Often referred to as 'the Hawaii of Scotland', Tiree attracts people from across the globe for kitesurfing, windsurfing, surfing and paddleboarding. Compared to much of Scotland, Tiree has a reasonably mild climate; it is one of the sunniest places in the whole of the UK and the ocean is gently warmed by the passing Gulf Stream. So, with sunshine, waves and warm(ish) water . . . there was no way we could write a book about Scotland's blue spaces without mentioning the island.

In terms of surfing, Tiree juts out into the North Atlantic with nothing but ocean separating it from the Americas. Therefore, its west and south coasts are perfectly positioned to attract some pretty big North Atlantic swells. Tiree, however, is also renowned for being incredibly windy; the prevailing wind blows onshore from the south-west, so for perfect surf conditions with an offshore wind and large Atlantic swell, a few stars do have to align. When they do, Tiree can be a world-class surfing destination. A great starting point on any surf trip here is Balevullin beach, where you will find family-run surf company Blackhouse Watersports, who are a great source of local knowledge on the conditions.

Tiree is famed as one of the best windsurfing destinations in Europe. This wee island even plays host to the Wave Classic, the world's longest-standing professional windsurfing competition. The windier months of the year in Tiree tend to be during springtime and early autumn, making this a

superb destination for more advanced sailors at this time of year. Comparatively, the calmer summer months of July and August are great for those just beginning to learn. Kitesurfing has also dramatically increased in popularity on Tiree over recent years.

The island has something for everyone, from calm shallow bays on the east coast, perfect for wild swimming, to huge open beaches with lots of swell on the west coast, all within a few minutes' drive of each other.

For paddleboarders and swimmers, when the wind drops there are a plethora of options, from exploring the more remote north coast to taking in the large sandy bays of the east coast. When I visited Tiree, the weather only allowed me to paddleboard once. One morning close to the end of

the trip we woke early in our campervan close to Gott Bay on the eastern side of the island to find that the wind had finally dropped. It was now or never to get on the water. I pumped up my board and headed down to the beach for what turned out to be one of the most glorious sunrise paddles of my life.

Tiree is the land of big skies and when the sky looks good, it looks really good. On this island you get the most amazing sunrises and sunsets, but even more magical than the daytime vistas on Tiree are the nighttime ones. Neighbouring island Coll has been designated an official Dark Sky Community, which guarantees you clear views of the night sky unspoilt by light pollution. Tiree doesn't have the same accolade, but there is little light pollution generated by this small community perched out in the Atlantic. The stars on a clear night are simply mind-blowing.

If you love watersports, Tiree needs to be added to your bucket list. The possibilities for water-based adventure here are endless. No matter the conditions, you will easily find a way to soak up some of that blue health.

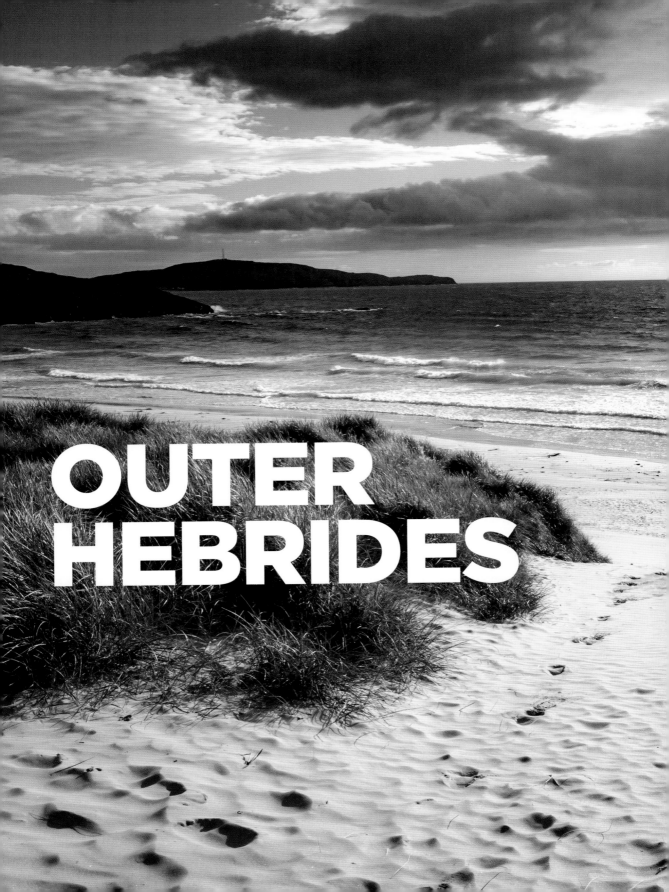

OUTER
HEBRIDES

VATERSAY

Activities	Surfing, swimming, kayaking, paddleboarding
Experience level	* *
Environment	Ocean
Start point	Car park between two main beaches
Carry time	5–10 mins
Public transport	Bus connections from Barra
OS map	452

Lying directly below the island of Barra is the most southerly inhabited island of the Outer Hebrides archipelago, Vatersay. This island is a literal paradise on a calm, warm day and a wild, raging land when the weather rolls in.

Vatersay is one of my favourite islands in the Outer Hebrides and I count myself lucky to have visited it more than once. The first time, the Atlantic Ocean roared, with gigantic white horses crashing onto the beach, the wind raged, and the rain hammered down. This island felt alive and raw,

warning me that it wasn't the day to explore its blue spaces. However, on my return visit the island was a much more hospitable beast, allowing us to surf, swim and explore its coastline.

In 1990, a causeway was finished over the narrow sound of Vatersay, connecting this isolated island to its more populated neighbour, Barra. This causeway meant better access to social services, shops, a daily postal service, refuse collection and much more for the locals.

Whilst researching this island, I found a

newspaper article from the *Chicago Tribune*, of all places. It stated that each year, before the building of the causeway, a bull would swim from Barra to Vatersay to 'spend a blissful summer with his 60 or so mates' – their words not mine! This bull would then complete the return swim to Barra in autumn. However, in 1987 the prized bull unfortunately drowned during the swim, leaving local farmers devastated and in debt. Maybe this had something to do with the causeway construction starting a year later?

Vatersay pinches in at the waist, where the ocean has eroded away the land. This has created two large bays with a narrow strip of land down the middle where the road weaves through. On the westerly side of the road you have the beach of Traigh Shiar and on the easterly side you have Traigh a Bhaigh, two beaches in very close proximity but with very different characteristics.

The beach to the west is exposed to the full force of the Atlantic Ocean, with no land to break its path until you reach the Americas. This is a great surfing and windsurfing destination, depending on the conditions. Here you will find crystal-clear water, empty waves, glorious white sand and often the local herd of cows (descendants of the prized bull perhaps?) casually grazing on seaweed and checking the surf conditions. In comparison, the beach to the east is often flat as a millpond, facing towards the mainland of Scotland and much less affected by the Atlantic swells and prevailing winds.

We parked in the small road-side car park between the two beaches, where we noted a sign that said overnight parking is permitted with a donation into the honesty box. Unfortunately, you can't see the beach from here, so we had to simply hope for some surfable waves on the western beach before clambering into our wetsuits. We were led through the sand dunes on a faint path lined with flowering machair – we had decided to visit the Hebrides in late spring, when this beautiful sight occurs. On reaching the beach, there was not a soul to be seen. It is a fabulous and common occurrence to have a Hebridean beach to yourself; however, caution must be taken when entering the blue spaces of these isolated islands. Help, if there is any, is a long way away.

After a fun surf in some messy island waves, observed by some cows who looked less than impressed by our efforts, we dropped the surfboards back at the van and ran across to the easterly beach in our wetsuits for a swim. There wasn't even a ripple on the water on this side of the island. We messed about in the calm water, behaving like children in a swimming pool, with handstands, shoulder fights and attempts to re-enact that famous Johnny and Baby lift from *Dirty Dancing*. This was until Rachel spotted a large and intimidating electric blue jellyfish on her underwater camera and we quickly exited the sea! Don't let this put you off, though. It quickly drifted away and, from our observations, it didn't seem to have any other jelly friends.

Vatersay is an isolated, wild island, fabulous for a variety of watersports. A small slice of Scottish paradise when you get the weather and an invigorating experience when you don't.

CASTLEBAY AND KISIMUL CASTLE, BARRA

Activities	Paddleboarding, kayaking
Experience level	★ ★ ★
Environment	Ocean
Start point	Car park at the marina
Carry time	2 minutes
Public transport	Calmac ferry from Oban
OS map	452

Barra lies at the southern end of the archipelago of the Outer Hebrides. At roughly 60 square kilometres, what this island lacks in size it makes up for in its wild beauty and island charm. Most visitors' first taste of the island is the settlement of Castlebay, where the Calmac ferry arrives daily from Oban, bringing locals and tourists alike to its shores.

Castlebay has been the heart of Barra for its entire inhabited history. Located on the east side of the island, away from the roar of the Atlantic Ocean, it is a natural harbour. Protected on three sides by hills and moorland, its neighbouring island, Vatersay, offers some protection to the south. One of the first sights to meet you as you sail into the bay is Kisimul Castle. Its Gaelic name is Caisteal Chiosmuil, which translates to 'castle of the rock of the small bay'. Built in the 1400s, the castle does indeed sit on a rocky islet in the bay, the ancestral home of Clan MacNeil. Barra has been the heartland of this clan for more than a thousand years, with the castle being occupied by clan chiefs for centuries. Today, Kisimul Castle is in the care of Historic Scotland, who pay

the very reasonable annual rent of £1 and a bottle of whisky to the 47th clan chief, Rory MacNeil.

Castlebay is a fantastic blue space to explore via kayak or paddleboard. Head out on a calm day to investigate its rocky shore, ancient castle and hidden inlets, all with the backdrop of the rolling hills of Barra. For this trip, we joined the team from Clearwater Paddling to explore the bay by sea kayak. Clearwater Paddling are a family-run kayaking adventure company based in Castlebay itself but who run tours across the Outer Hebrides packed full of local knowledge. Our launch point was a large slipway next to the marina, where you will also find a good-sized car park.

We pointed our kayaks south towards Vatersay, hugging the coastline as we paddled. We explored the causeway, which was built in 1990 to link the two neighbouring islands by road for the first time. Near the causeway we were lucky enough to see dozens of seals popping up around us as they fed on the high tide. The waters around Barra are rich with sea life. We may have only encountered seals on this journey, but sightings of sea otters, porpoises and

dolphins are common, with the occasional basking shark and orca pod too.

After retracing our paddle strokes back into the main expanse of the bay, we headed straight for the castle. Looking up at this towering fortress from sea level is a dizzying experience. It is always particularly special to experience these monuments of Scottish history from the water, a vantage that few get to enjoy.

Kisimul Castle is the only remaining medieval castle in the Outer Hebrides; it was lovingly restored during the 1900s to represent some of its former glory and protect its history.

As we were exploring the castle inlet, the Calmac ferry launched from the port en route to the mainland. Calmac ferries are an icon of the islands of Scotland, and it was quite an experience to view this huge metal beast from the water, and then to bounce through its wake.

The natural harbour of Castlebay and Kisimul Castle itself offer a reasonably protected and accessible blue space to explore via kayak or paddleboard, with great facilities close by.

TRAIGH EAIS & TRAIGH MHOR, BARRA

Activities	Surfing, swimming
Experience level	★ ★ ★ ★
Environment	Ocean
Start point	Car park at airport
Carry time	10-15 mins
Public transport	Calmac ferry to Barra, W32 bus
OS map	452

At the northern tip of Barra, where the land narrows, you will find two glorious blue spaces lying back-to-back. On the wild west coast is Traigh Eais, a stunning expanse of golden sand open to the power of the Atlantic Ocean and often surfed. However, on the east coast lies its much more famous sister, Traigh Mhor – or, as it's better known, Barra airport beach.

To reach these beaches – if you are not arriving by air, that is – follow signs through the island to

Barra airport, where you will find a large car park and a cafe in the airport itself. Barra airport is an aeronautical marvel to experience: twice a day, flights come and go to Glasgow, but the cool thing is that these planes come and go on a runway that consists entirely of Traigh Mhor. The planes take off and land from the sand at low tide, then as the tide rises the runway is washed away. I haven't yet had the chance to take this flight, but one day I will need to bite the bullet. I can imagine just how amazing it would be to take off from the hustle and bustle of one of the UK's major cities and then land 1 hour 10 minutes later on the sands of this island heaven.

Crossing the road from the airport, you will see a gate in the fence and a path leading towards sand dunes ahead. Take this path to visit Traigh Mhor's wilder sister beach.

Traigh Eais is a huge golden stretch backed by dunes and is known as one of Barra's premier surfing beaches. That said, in this quiet corner of the world you are unlikely to meet many other surfers in the water. For the best conditions, this beach needs a north-westerly swell combined with an offshore east/south-easterly wind. As you approach the beach there are various signs warning you of strong undercurrents and rips. Traigh Eais is exposed to the full force of the Atlantic Ocean and on big swell days many rip tides can appear along this stretch – care and experience is needed for those wanting to use this blue space.

We had arrived into Castlebay via the Calmac ferry the night before and the next morning were greeted with low hanging clouds that refused to shift throughout the day. However, as we walked through the dunes to reach Traigh Eais the clouds finally began to lift and Barra revealed itself to us, masked in glorious golden-hour light. We had the whole beach to ourselves and, even though the conditions weren't great for surfing, spent a blissful evening swimming in the messy waves of the Atlantic Ocean and watching the summer sun set over the water.

Traigh Eais is an incredible beach and well worth a visit. But do take care when entering the water here, which can be dangerous. As always, when in doubt, stay out.

THE PRINCE'S STRAND, ERISKAY

Activities	Swimming, paddleboarding, kayaking
Experience level	* *
Environment	Ocean
Start point	Car park at the ferry terminal or layby
Carry time	10 mins
Public transport	Calmac ferry to Eriskay
OS map	452

Eriskay is one of the highlights of any journey through the Outer Hebrides. Nestled between Barra and South Uist, this small island has a lot to shout about: beaches as white as any Caribbean island, ocean as blue as the Mediterranean, a great pub and even a native species of pony!

Eriskay has a population of around 140. The island stretches from north to south for just 3 miles, and from east to west for just over 1 mile. It wasn't until 2001 that a causeway was built to connect Eriskay and South Uist; this was part of a series of infrastructure developments aiming to link Eriskay by road to Berneray in the far north. Being able to drive this 60-mile route has had a huge impact on

the local population in terms of access to work, healthcare and education – as well as attracting tourists from all over the world to cycle, drive or even paddle this route.

The Eriskay blue space I chose is a beach known as the Prince's Strand. It's a stretch of pure white shell-sand and shallow water, with a backdrop of the mesmerising blue ocean. The beach is named after Bonnie Prince Charlie, as this is said to be the very spot where he first set foot on Scottish soil in July 1745. His intention was to restore the Stuart dynasty by taking the throne of Great Britain. The Bonnie Prince's attempts were ill-fated, and after his defeat at Culloden in 1746 he fled back to France, with

disastrous consequences for the Highland clans who had supported him and Gaelic culture as a whole. There is no physical sign or plaque to highlight this beach's history, apart from the clue in the name, also known locally as the Prince's Beach.

If you take the Calmac ferry from Barra to Eriskay, make sure you are on deck to witness the first glimpses of this beach. The Prince's Strand is a glorious sight, and an even better place to take a dip into the blue ocean. As you leave the ferry terminal, the beach is no more than 100 metres up the hill, with parking in a large layby on the left-hand side of the road or at the ferry terminal itself. Don't be tempted to just exit the ferry and push on with your journey north: stop here for a dip; you won't regret it.

We decided to take a swim here, as it was a little too windy for paddleboarding, but on a calm day this would make a lovely paddling destination and one I will be coming back for. With the small island of Lingay sitting comfortably on the horizon, we entered the clear water for a bracing swim and a brilliant welcome to Eriskay. Afterwards we whiled away an easy hour walking up and down this beautiful beach, even managing to spot a small pink cowrie shell nestled in the sand!

The Prince's Strand is a super-accessible beach right next to the road and ferry terminal, but a dip in the ocean here will do wonders for your mind, body and soul.

PETER'S PORT, BENBECULA

Activities	Paddleboarding, kayaking, swimming
Experience level	✶ ✶ ✶
Environment	Ocean and inlets
Start point	At port or along road
Carry time	Roadside
Public transport	N/A
OS map	453

Benbecula, sandwiched between North Uist and South Uist, is often overlooked by travellers, but there is a lot more to this small island than just a spot of land between the many causeways that link this part of the Hebrides together. There are plenty of opportunities here for exploring some unique blue spaces that differ from much of the rest of this archipelago. Benbecula boasts a watery landscape, with countless fresh and saltwater lochs dotting much of its surface to the east, and with the classic Hebridean open dunes and

shell-sand beaches lining the west.

The Outer Hebrides tends to draw you towards the west coast beaches, and for good reason – many of them are mind-bogglingly stunning – however, we were on the hunt for something a little different, a hidden gem, and when we got speaking to a local wild swimmer in a cafe on South Uist we knew we'd found what we were looking for.

This intriguing location on the east coast of Benbecula, good for paddleboarding and swimming at high tide, is named Peter's Port. Unlike most of

our Hebridean locations, this one had a name I could pronounce!

We turned off the main A865 road and onto a minor single-track lane that weaved through this watery land. As we drove over causeways, small bridges and interconnecting tiny islands, it felt like we may have been sent on a wild-goose chase by our new friend – this was until the road finally ran out and we arrived at a small boat yard with a couple of containers, tons of stacked creel baskets and a few spooky-looking old boats moored on the water. Although there was not a soul in sight, this was obviously a working port and not a tourist attraction. We parked our big blue van as out of the way as we could (there is not much available parking here and no designated bays. If you do choose to visit, make sure to park as conservatively as possible, or even further up the road away from the port, in order to respect the people who work in this area) and began unloading our kit.

There is a large slipway down to the water's edge where you can launch a paddleboard or kayak from; this would also make a great place to swim from at high tide. Once on the water, there are many options for paddling: you can head out into the bay directly in front of the slipway to explore the countless rocky islands poking above the surface, or you could turn inland, where interconnecting creeks entice you around every corner. We visited this area on a rising neap tide and still managed to work our way quite far inland, connecting the deeper water. However, I would love to experience this landscape on a high spring tide, or even attempt to paddle north into Loch Chearabhaigh itself. This paddle is a true adventure, with so many options for exploring. With that in mind, take a map with you; it could be very easy to get lost in this watery maze and even get stuck, as the tide drains out.

This environment was unlike anything we experienced elsewhere in the Hebrides, an archipelago renowned for its vast sandy beaches. The complex weaving of rivers, rocky islets and dense patches of seaweed felt otherworldly and made for an exciting paddle.

As we were driving back from Peter's Port along the single-track road, we spotted a mother otter in the water with her baby resting on her chest. We stopped the van and managed to quietly watch this splendid scene for a few moments before they sensed our presence and dove back underwater. A beautiful sighting at the end of another epic *Blue Scotland* adventure.

Peter's Port is far off the beaten track and offers a true exploration of this scattered blue landscape.

HOSTA, NORTH UIST

Activities	Surfing
Experience level	✴ ✴ ✴ ✴ ✴
Environment	Ocean
Start point	Car park behind dunes
Carry time	5 mins
Public transport	Bus connections from Lochmaddy
OS map	454

Nestled on the west coast of North Uist is one of the Outer Hebrides' most famous surf spots: Hosta. Here you will find a beautiful white shell-sand beach backed by high sand dunes and acres of machair, as well as some pretty consistent North Atlantic swell.

Hosta is notorious amongst the inhabitants of North Uist. Local non-surfers will warn you not to enter the water here – over the years there have unfortunately been several drownings at this beach.

It is renowned for strong rip currents that can easily catch out people using this blue space. Local surfers, on the other hand, will tell you to come here during the winter months, when the swell is often double overhead. My recommendation? Know your own limits and only enter the water here if you are an experienced surfer. If you are, this is a truly awesome spot for you to visit. If you are at all apprehensive, there are plenty of other beginner-friendly surf beaches nearby to try. I would not recommend

swimming or paddleboarding here; there are other options for this along the coastline.

Even if you don't plan on entering the water at Hosta, it is still very much worth a visit on any tour of North Uist. The beach is simply stunning. There is plenty of choice for walking and cycling in the area, and from the safety of the sand it is a great place to absorb the blue health benefits of this island.

Hosta is a north-west facing beach, capable of holding huge swell rolling in from the North Atlantic. It is best surfed on a rising mid to high tide. The infamous rip is at the north end of the beach by the rocks and can appear even in moderate-sized swell. This rip can be used by experienced surfers as a quick option to get out behind the breaking waves. Hosta is one of the few Hebridean surf spots to have its own Magicseaweed surf forecast – it's handy to have an advance view of what the waves might be like. North Uist has a small but hardy surf community of around 20 people who, in my experience, are incredibly friendly and psyched to share their local spots with the handful of visitors who come to surf on their island. When the surf is good at Hosta, you will also find surfers from Harris and Lewis making the pilgrimage south.

I have surfed at Hosta on two separate visits to the Outer Hebrides, both occasions in small, sloppy summer waves. I would love to have the opportunity to return and witness this coastline going off in a big winter swell. Make no mistake, I'm unlikely to have the guts or required skill to go in, but I would love to watch the locals from the safety of the dunes.

In terms of access, you can follow the main road north up the west coast. You will see a sign on your right to Hosta village and a sign on your left to a parking and picnic area; turn left here and follow a dirt track around to a small parking area, enough for six to eight cars. You will see that a lot of the machair here is fenced off to protect it. Machair across the Hebrides has been ruined in recent years by the influx of tourists driving and parking on this delicate habitat. The machair around Hosta is home to a variety of wildflowers, including a very rare orchid, and ground-nesting birds; it is particularly vulnerable to destruction by vehicles. With this in mind, please be cautious. Only drive on existing tracks and park in the existing designated area.

Hosta is a beautiful beach and an awesome surf destination throughout the year, but it's best reserved for more experienced surfers.

SCOLPAIG, NORTH UIST

Activities	Paddleboarding, kayaking, swimming
Experience level	* *
Environment	Ocean
Start point	Unpaved access track near Scolpaig Tower
Carry time	0.6 miles
Public transport	Bus connections from Lochmaddy
OS map	454

As with so many of the best blue spaces we found whilst in the Outer Hebrides, Scolpaig was recommended to us by a friendly local with excellent knowledge of the best spots for swimming. So if you do manage to pay a visit to this beautiful swimming or paddleboarding spot, spare a thought for Duncan at the Creel Yard, who really was a fount of knowledge!

This isn't the easiest beach to access, but it is well worth persevering for the chance to swim in this sheltered spot. There is space for one or two cars parked carefully to preserve the machair off an access track on the A865; you'll know you're in the right spot when approaching from the south, as there's a red postbox on the left just before you reach the track. Otherwise keep your eyes peeled for the distinctive form of Scolpaig Tower, which rises from a small islet in Loch Scolpaig and can be seen from the road.

From here, the walk is just over half a mile down an easy track. The time passes very quickly as you head directly past the tower, which is nearly 200 years old. After this, you pass through a small cluster of abandoned dwellings in a state of ruin; we may have upped our pace when heading back to the car as daylight was waning. Despite the beautiful scenery, this is not an insignificant carry for a paddleboard and so this location maybe best suited for swimming.

Scolpaig is known in the wild swimming community for its stunning tidal pool. Accessed at low tide, this is a natural swimming pool with a gentle rock slope leading down to the water – perfect for a splash-about amongst beautiful surroundings. This protected spot with clear water is great for swimmers with limited experience, as the low tide cuts off the pool from the sea, ensuring no currents are likely to catch you off-guard.

For the more confident swimmer, we would highly recommend Scolpaig beach itself. This bay is still very protected and provides a sheltered spot. Before we got into the water, we walked along the headland to the very edges of the cliff and watched the waves thrash against the rocks below. However, when we got down to the beach the might of the

Atlantic had been lulled into a gentle ebb and flow, protected by the rocky coastline which curves round the bay, meaning access to the sea was very straightforward.

This coastline is known for its sea caves, but also for its sea otters, so we kept our eyes peeled as we made our way over the machair to the beach. Once we had set foot on the sand all thoughts of otters were forgotten as we stared out into the strangest optical illusion. As you swim out from the beach, the wild ocean can be seen through a small gap in the rocks where part of the headland becomes an island when the tide rises. Through this gap the waves almost seem as though they're about to come sweeping through and crash over your head! Thankfully, the hidden bridge connecting the island to the mainland acts as a barrier, soothing the tempestuous waves before they reach you.

Once you have overcome the initial hesitation at this sight, there is plenty to explore up and down the cliff face, much of which can only be seen from the water. As you swim along it feels as though you're moving through a different world, the juxtaposition of thick weed and golden sand beneath the surface changing the colour and feel of the water around you. After clearing the weed the sea becomes crystal clear for several metres below you – despite our best duck-diving efforts, we were unable to reach the bottom, which was clearly visible from the surface.

Although Scolpaig doesn't have the notoriety of the nearby tidal pool or the miles of golden sand that draw you to other spots in the Hebrides, it is not one to be overlooked. Our advice? Take a packed lunch and a snorkel; with so many caves, pools and rocky islets to explore, this is an incredible spot to appreciate the nature that abounds in the Outer Hebrides.

SOLLAS, NORTH UIST

Activities	Swimming, surfing
Experience level	✱ ✱ ✱ ✱
Environment	Ocean
Start point	Co-op, Sollas village
Carry time	30–50 mins
Public transport	Bus connections from Lochmaddy
OS map	454

The beach at Sollas is one of the finest on the island of North Uist. Remote, quiet and raw, this crescent-shaped expanse of sand, dunes and open machair faces north-west, looking out to the powerful Atlantic Ocean. Sollas is a superb surfing destination for beginners and advanced surfers alike, and a fun place to have a swim amongst the crashing Atlantic waves.

Our beach is located on the west flank of the awesomely shaped Àird a' Mhòrain peninsula. These days, the beach is mostly referred to as Sollas, but you may note that on a map it is labelled Traigh Iar, with Sollas being the name of the nearest settlement.

Sollas beach is not the easiest to access. It lies about a mile from the nearest road. However, I can promise you that the trek down to the sand is worth it. The safest way to reach this epic beach is to park near the Co-op shop in Sollas village and hike; this way, the machair and local wildlife are protected. Here you will also find a small community space that commemorates the clearance of crofters from the land. In 1849, more than 600 inhabitants of Sollas were forcefully cleared from their land by Lord MacDonald. Many townsfolk emigrated across the

Atlantic to Cape Breton, Nova Scotia. One Hebridean settlement there was even named Sollas (now known as Woodbine).

By the time we parked up in the village, it was late afternoon and we had spent the whole day exploring North Uist. The idea of carrying our surfboards and wetsuits on the mile hike down to the beach was unappealing, to say the least. However, we had been told by a local that Sollas beach was not one to be missed. We took the main track opposite the Co-op, past some houses on the left and through a metal gate. Soon the machair fields spread out on each side of the track and the sound of chirping ground-nesting birds filled the air, as they danced through the flowers. We finally reached the sharp, pointed dunes of Sollas sands and found a path leading us through, popping out slap bang in the middle of the beach.

The sheer size of Sollas totally blew us away. White shell-sand extended away from us in each direction. Once again, we were the only people in sight – we had another glorious Hebridean beach to ourselves. After soaking this place in for a few minutes, Tegan and I jumped into our wetsuits,

grabbed our boards and headed down to the water's edge. Dozens of orange-legged, orange-beaked oystercatchers scattered the beach, clearly enjoying an early dinner.

The surfing at Sollas is much more beginner-friendly than nearby Hosta; however, this beach is still capable of holding a large swell, with various left and right peaks. Sollas juts out directly into the Atlantic, meaning it is one of, if not the, most

consistent surf beaches on the island. On small swell days it would be an invigorating place to take a swim and you will most likely have the place to yourself. Do be mindful of rip currents as the swell grows and consider the isolation of this place; you will likely end up in Nova Scotia before help arrives.

Sollas takes a bit of effort to reach, but the reward of endless sand, empty waves and pure uninhibited blue health is there to be reaped.

SCARISTA, HARRIS

Activities	Surfing, swimming, paddleboarding, kayaking
Experience level	✳ ✳ ✳
Environment	Ocean
Start point	Layby on A859
Carry time	20 minutes
Public transport	Bus connections from Tarbert and Leverburgh
OS map	455

Scarista beach, on the south-west tip of Harris, is an example of the Outer Hebrides at its finest. Here you will find a backdrop of the rounded mountains of South Harris easing into machair-covered dunes, fine golden sand, clear turquoise water and peeling surfable waves rolling in from the North Atlantic. To blue space enthusiasts, Scarista beach is probably the closest place to paradise you will find on a Scottish coastline.

I have been lucky enough to visit Scarista a few times and, as you will probably tell from my introductory paragraph above, this is by far my favourite beach on Harris, if not in the entire Outer Hebrides. When the surfing is good on Harris, it is always good at Scarista. The beach faces north-west, open to the forces of the North Atlantic. Unlike other beaches on Harris, there is limited protection from the geography of nearby islands and headlands here, meaning that the waves in autumn and winter can be giants.

Scarista beach tends to be much quieter than many of the other honey pot beaches on Harris, mainly due to its mile-long walk in from the road. There are various access points to this beach, but we chose to park in a large layby on the ocean side of the A859 – look out for the road sign for Sgarasta

Bheag/Scaristaveg at one end of the layby. At the other end of the layby, you will find a gate and a signpost reading 'Scarista 1 mile'; head through this and follow the path ahead. As you reach the sand dunes, look out for another gate up on your left, with a small plaque for the Hebridean Way. Continue through this instead of being drawn into the sand dunes. More than once I have followed the enticing track into the dunes and got stuck behind a system of fences!

The mile-long walk into Scarista couldn't be more worth it, even if you are laden with heavy boards and kit. This humongous sandy stretch sprawls out in front of you, gently descending into a stunning turquoise ocean. Due to its sheer size, even on a busy day Scarista feels quiet and remote. There is plenty of space on the sand for beach goers, and plenty of waves to go around in the line-up.

Scarista is a popular spot for surfing in the Outer Hebrides, and by Hebridean standards this means there are often never more than a handful of surfers in the water at once. It is a reasonably safe beach break, with various peaks the whole way along the shore, but do watch out for strong rips, even on small swell days. Scarista also has its own Magicseaweed surf report, so you can get an idea of what the waves might be like before undertaking the walk. When the swell drops off, as often happens in the summer months, Scarista is a brilliant beach for swimming and paddleboarding. Don't be surprised to see seals bobbing around in the water with you or eagles soaring above the machair.

Scarista is the epitome of epic blue space in Scotland, with its large stretch of sand and its glorious backdrop and remote feel. Head here to soak up a little bit of Scottish heaven.

LUSKENTYRE, HARRIS

Activities	Swimming, paddleboarding, kayaking
Experience level	*
Environment	Ocean
Start point	Luskentyre beach car park
Carry time	Less than 5 mins (approx. 50 m)
Public transport	Bus connections from Tarbert and Leverburgh
OS map	455

When people think of the Outer Hebrides, many minds go straight to Luskentyre. Indeed, when people think of iconic places in Scotland, or even just of spectacular beaches, Luskentyre comes up time and again. It is believed by many to be the jewel in the crown of outstanding Scottish and Hebridean beaches, and for this reason its reputation precedes it.

Harris was our penultimate stop on our tour of the Outer Hebrides, meaning that by the time we arrived at Luskentyre we had sampled some of the finest blue spaces on Barra, Eriskay, North and South Uist, and many of the smaller islands in between. Having not been to Luskentyre before, I was struggling to believe that it would match up to the glorious spots we had already visited.

Upon arrival it is clear that the local community trust has invested time, energy and money into ensuring that the infrastructure can cater to the many tourists who visit the beach (although the term 'many' is relative; what is considered busy by Hebridean standards would be seen as deserted in many other parts of the world). The car park is tarmacked and of a decent size to accommodate plenty of visitors. It also houses a toilet block.

However, as soon as you leave the car park and take the short walk down to the beach it becomes immediately apparent why this spot is so special to so many. The vast expanse of golden sand leads down to crystal-clear water that glitters in invitation, but rather than the ocean stretching into a distant flat horizon, as we're used to, towering mountains rise above the sea from North Harris on the right, whilst the island of Taransay lies in front of you, sheltering the beach from much of the Atlantic swell.

The abundance of wildlife that we had seen in the Hebrides was very much present on Luskentyre. We arrived at the beach on a mid, dropping tide, meaning that it would be several hours before the sea once again returned to the high-tide line. With this in mind, we decided to attempt to repatriate several star fish that were lying on the drying sand under the warm sun, carefully popping them back into the sea in the hope they'd fight another day. The rockpools on the right-hand side of the beach were also host to an impressive diversity of wildlife,

and I found myself cursing (yet again) that I didn't have my snorkel with me.

The beautiful stretch of sand and amazing clarity of the water are not the main draws of Luskentyre. Make no mistake, they are incredible, but their like can be found up and down the Hebrides. Rather, what sets Luskentyre apart is the mountainous skyline that dwarfs you as you swim. There is a unique sense of awe and reverence that I feel when I'm in the mountains, the knowledge that we're so very small in an enormous universe.

Experiencing this precise feeling whilst being in such a remarkable blue space was the merging of two very important parts of my life, and it is hard to put into words.

I could continue to write for several pages, trying hard to articulate the majesty and awe that is invoked by Luskentyre, but I'm sure I would never be able to do it justice. Rather I recommend that you visit and take plenty of time to bask in the presence of both mountains and blue space – it's a very compelling combination.

HUISINIS, HARRIS

Activities	Swimming, paddleboarding, kayaking
Experience level	* *
Environment	Ocean
Start point	Huisinis Gateway car park
Carry time	N/A (just cross the road and you're on the beach!)
Public transport	Bus connections from Tarbert
OS map	456

Huisinis is a small, secluded, sandy paradise found at the end of a 12-mile-long single-track road. The drive to get here truly is epic, full of hairpin bends, steep climbs and blind summits. The terrain itself requires a cautious driver, but your speed is limited further by the herds of sheep and Highland cattle that litter the road, as well as the intrepid cyclists who brave this tricky route.

Although the destination is truly superb, we cannot emphasise enough how much we recommend enjoying the journey. We found at one point the Highland cattle were not perturbed at all by our van, leaving us to sit stationary for quite some considerable amount of time whilst they moved around us, searching for the juiciest patch of grass.

On the route you will pass through the Amhuinnsuidhe estate, the old stone castle and beautifully manicured grounds standing in stark juxtaposition to the rugged countryside you've just come through. Our recommendation is to stop off at the Amhuinnsuidhe Castle shop; it's operated on an honesty basis, so you can drop in and purchase locally reared venison steaks and burgers fresh from the estate. The venison burgers we picked up made one of the finest meals we ate during our time on the Hebrides.

As you crest the final hill, the golden sands of Huisinis start to appear in the distance. There is still perhaps 1 mile to go until you're in the bay properly, but on the approach you'll notice a small campervan

parking site on your right-hand side. There's electric hook up available here (April–October) but the parking area is very small and works on a first come, first served basis, so we recommend arriving early if you plan to stay overnight and require the electric hook up. Otherwise there is another parking area further down the road beside the beach and the visitor centre. This car park doesn't have electric hook up, but still offers chemical waste disposal, fresh water and recycling.

It's not often in a book focusing on blue spaces I would dedicate an entire paragraph to a visitor centre, but the Huisinis Gateway building really is spectacular. From an amenities point of view, it provides clean toilets and showers for guests (the showers are coin-operated), and a warm, dry look-out room, with stellar views over the beach and indoor picnic space if you're unlucky enough to visit on a rainy day. However, for me the standout of the Gateway building is the information boards on the walls, which share incredible amounts of local knowledge covering the history of the area and the flora and fauna that can be found nearby. All this work has been undertaken by the North Harris Trust, who have done a truly incredible job building infrastructure that protects the local environment from damage through footfall but allows them to share their wee corner of paradise with the many tourists who visit this incredible place.

Huisinis beach at first glance may seem rather diminutive in comparison to the vast spaces of some of its more famous counterparts on the island, however its remote location and plentiful wildlife make it very special. There really is something for everyone here: it's an incredible spot for wild swimmers, with clear blue, shallow water across the bay; over on the far right-hand side are some rock

pools teeming with wildlife – we were particularly jealous of those we spotted who had thought to bring snorkels and will certainly bring them on our next trip. Even from the beach and my paddleboard I managed to spot plenty of starfish that I would love to see from a closer vantage point. For paddleboarders, the opportunity to paddle around this protected bay with so much wildlife is really special.

Huisinis beach itself is wonderful, but it's truly the entire experience of travelling down the long, winding road to such a secluded spot that is full of nature and has been so well protected by the North Harris Trust that makes this blue space so special.

TRAIGH MHEILEIN, HARRIS

Activities	Swimming
Experience level	* * *
Environment	Ocean
Start point	Huisinis Gateway car park
Carry time	40 mins on a steep cliff path
Public transport	Bus connections from Tarbert to Huisinis, then walk
OS map	456

Traigh Mheilein is the bonus wild swim add-on to our entry on Huisinis – so please do read that first, as it contains lots of useful information about travel and access. Prior to our arrival at Huisinis we had already decided we'd park the van and stay the night, giving us precious extra hours in this awesome corner of the Hebrides. Although that time would have been well spent in Huisinis, I'm so glad we decided to explore slightly further afield and make the trip to Traigh Mheilein.

The route can be found as part of a longer venture on the Walk Highlands website but is very straightforward. To protect the machair and not disturb any ground-nesting birds, it's important that you stick to existing paths and follow the instructions on the signage. The route branches off from the main road just behind the Huisinis Gateway building, although it's well worth stopping off there, as the signage contains lots of interesting information about the island of Scarp – more on that later!

From here, a well-worn but paved road takes you towards the coast on the northern side of the Huisinis peninsula, closer to the aforementioned Scarp. Just before you reach the sea, a worn path on the right leads off towards a stile that marks the beginning of a clearer path that meanders up the

cliff. It is this route that will take you towards the beautiful Traigh Mheilein.

As the path crests the cliff, the bright golden sand of Traigh Mheilein appears in the distance. Our progress was fairly slow as we attempted to keep one eye on the path in front of us and one eye firmly on the channel of water between ourselves and Scarp, hoping to catch a glimpse of a seal, dolphin or even a minke whale. I was also attempting to soak up Rachel's excellent knowledge of seabirds in order to start identifying a few myself. Our leisurely progress allowed for true enjoyment of this beautiful walk.

When we finally descended towards the beach it became clear that the sliver of sand we had seen from the cliff path was only a small sample of what was on offer: the beach extends round the corner and into the distance. As you head down the initial stretch of beach, there's a large piece of old, ruined machinery that catches the eye. We spent a long time pondering what it could be, as it seemed far too big to have been washed up so high above the tide line, even in the most vicious of winter storms. We were later advised that these were the remnants of an ill-fated attempt to introduce a rocket-powered postal service between Harris and the island of Scarp back when it was still inhabited – it's a story worth looking up!

We made our way much further down the beach before heading into the water for a swim. The channel between Traigh Mheilein and Scarp is known for its strong, unforgiving current – one of the reasons (aside from the long hike!) that this beach isn't suitable for paddleboarding. We finally entered the water at the far end of the beach, where a large sand bar juts out, protecting you from the current and creating a large shallow pool to swim in. We waded out for perhaps 10 minutes with the water never getting past our waists before we took the plunge.

Another great perk of this beach is the large sand dunes that offer some protection from the biting wind. We were incredibly lucky on this trip that the weather really was fantastic, but despite this it was still Scotland in June, so any shelter when changing after getting out of the water was very much appreciated!

Traigh Mheilein is everything you could hope for in a Hebridean beach: beautiful, untouched and isolated. We had the entire beach to ourselves and were able to look back and see only our footprints whilst we sat and took in the great expanse of mountains, sky and ocean, without feeling any of the pressures of time that usually accompany everything that we do.

Traigh Mheilein offers visitors a little slice of solitude – the exclusivity granted by not being able to reach the beach by road only adds to the experience. It was the perfect way to spend a day.

TRAIGH GHEARADHA, LEWIS

Activities	Paddleboarding, kayaking, swimming
Experience level	★ ★ ★ ★ ★
Environment	Ocean
Start point	Car park above the beach, just off the B895
Carry time	10 mins (from car park to beach)
Public transport	Bus connections from Stornoway
OS map	460

Traigh Ghearadha, also known as Garry Beach, lies on the north-east coast of Lewis, close to the village of North Tolsta. Garry Beach was one of the final stops on our trip to the Outer Hebrides. Having spent two weeks making our way from Vatersay and Barra in the south all the way through to Lewis in the north, we had been spoiled by the many miles of golden beaches that we had visited on the way. Despite having the same fine sand that you associate with the Outer Hebrides, Garry Beach was geologically very different to the wide-open blue spaces that we were used to, and offered us an adventure all of its own.

We had arrived at the car park above Garry Beach late in the day, just as the sun was starting to weaken, as it tends to do during long summer evenings. Although we were going to stay in the van overnight and hit the water in the morning, we couldn't resist a quick recce. Who can say no to a chance to squidge their toes into the sand and spend time in a glorious blue space?

The short walk down from the car park to the beach takes you along a sandy path that cuts through the grass past a loch – there were an abundance of different birds on the loch when we

visited, including many wild geese with young goslings, so we gave them a wide berth.

The beautiful thing about arriving the evening before was that we got to explore the beach at low tide. The towering sea stacks that rise above the surface of the ocean were exposed, meaning we could walk around them, tilting our heads back to gaze up at the gulls circling above them. This granted us a rare opportunity to know precisely what was hidden deep under the surface when we took to the water in the morning.

After a decent walk exploring along the edge of the cliffs in preparation for our trip the next day, we headed back to the van and after two long weeks of adventuring it didn't take much for us to quickly fall into a deep sleep. Our awakening came suddenly and very, very early with the feeling of an external force moving the entire van. Convinced that someone was trying to break in and eat our breakfast, Tegan dropped down from the pop-top bed to investigate.

What she found was not a hungry burglar but a small herd of Highland cattle, who had noticed the bike rack on the rear door of the van and determined that it would make an excellent bum-

scratching post. Their vigour had caused the whole van to shake and despite our best efforts they were not to be deterred, meaning we had little choice but to abandon sleep and get ready for the day.

Garry Beach is separated from the long, sandy stretches of neighbouring Traigh Mhor by a small headland. We had read several reports that had described the beauty of the sea stacks and cave system on the small headland, and we set out to explore it. Keen for the challenge, Tegan opted to swim the route, while I chose the paddleboard. Initially this put her at an advantage, as she was able to cut through the breaking waves quickly to the open ocean, whilst I kept to my knees for the first several metres in order to make it through the white water.

Throughout our journey around Scotland's blue spaces, we have always preferred to err on the side of caution and safety. This trip was no different. Although we knew that the sporty swell was well within our limits and skills, we kept our distance from the sea stacks to ensure we wouldn't be caught close to the rocks – particularly as Tegan was swimming. Yet this allowed us to observe the geology of the headland as a whole, rather than in parts. The ragged stacks and cliffs rising from the water really made for a remarkable sight as we paddled along.

Not long after, we turned the corner into Traigh Mhor, a beach that is more reminiscent of your archetypal Hebridean shore, with an expanse of sand that reaches to the headland in the distance. As we headed in through the shallow water, we were afforded the chance to try our hand at surfing our paddleboards into the beach – a skill that could still do with some honing!

There is something to be said for this north-easterly corner of Lewis. Its towering sea stacks and rugged geology may be different from the vast sandy beaches of western Harris, but Garry Beach, Traigh Mhor and the headland that separates them have a magic all of their own.

ST KILDA

Activities	Swimming
Experience level	✶ ✶
Environment	Ocean
Start point	Village Bay
Carry time	None
Public transport	Boat trip to St Kilda
OS map	460

Erupting out of the North Atlantic some 50 to 60 million years ago was the volcanic mass of St Kilda. Over millennia, it was split by the power of the ocean into the archipelago we know today. St Kilda comprises the main island of Hirta, along with the smaller islands of Dùn, Boreray, Soy and the many pointed sea stacks that surround this archipelago. This small group of isolated islands are internationally recognised for their extensive seabird populations and famed for their near incomprehensible human history. I have never visited an island quite like St Kilda; stepping onto her shore is a humbling experience, and having the opportunity to swim in her waters is a real privilege.

For a chance to visit St Kilda, the weather needs to be near perfect to make the crossing to these isolated islands. On my 31st birthday, while on a trip to the Isle of Harris, the stars aligned and the

weather gods blessed us with the opportunity to visit this bucket-list destination. There are several boat companies that will take you from the Outer Hebrides or the Isle of Skye to St Kilda; we joined Kilda Cruises and set sail from Leverburgh harbour on board their small 12-person passenger boat. As we left the sheltered waters of the Isle of Harris and began bouncing over the North Atlantic swell, the wealth of wildlife in these waters began to reveal itself to us.

Beautiful yellow-headed gannets tracked our boat, adjusting their speed so that they could fly alongside us for a few moments. They were so close that you could appreciate their gigantic two-metre wingspan and see the brown tips of their wings beat the air. Glorious, chubby puffins sat on the water's surface and clumsily took to the air as our boat sped past. We spotted dolphins in our wake, the quickest glimpse of a minke whale and a mysterious lone black fin in the distance.

After a couple of hours on the water we got our first glimpse of St Kilda. Sharp, rocky islands jutting out of the vast blue horizon. The main island of Hirta is home to the highest sea cliffs in the UK,

rising to over 400 metres out of the ocean; these dramatic black cliffs make up an intimidating and alluring skyline as you approach across the water. We soon entered Village Bay, its smooth, semi-circular shape resembling an amphitheatre, with the island of Dùn to the south-east.

The first creatures to call St Kilda home after the last Ice Age must have been the seabirds, and today they flock in their hundreds of thousands to these plentiful waters and secure breeding sites each year. St Kilda is one of the most important habitats for breeding seabirds in the North Atlantic; this small archipelago supports an incredible 330,000 breeding pairs of 17 different bird species, meaning that at the height of the season it hosts around 1 million birds!

We were lucky to be visiting St Kilda at this time, and witnessed the spectacle of the UK's largest colony of puffins in flight. To me, puffins always look a little too bottom heavy to fly, but these orange-beaked birds put on quite a show. Resembling a swarm of bees, thousands upon thousands of them circled high above our boat. On these small islands you will also find 30 per cent of the UK's population

of northern gannets, who plunge into the waters at speeds of up to 60 miles per hour to fish. Other bird species here include huge populations of razorbills, kittiwakes, skuas and fulmars. The seabirds of St Kilda were by far the most concentrated mass of wildlife I have seen within the UK. One million seabirds breeding and feeding off this small archipelago is an incredible spectacle to behold.

The seabirds of St Kilda are intrinsically linked to the success of thousands of years of human habitation on this rocky outcrop in the Atlantic. Continuous human settlements here date back at least 2,000 years. However, archaeologists have found evidence of much older human activity on these islands, dating back almost 5,000 years. It isn't known if these were occasional visitors or more permanent island settlers. At its peak population, St Kilda would have been home to close to 200 people. A small, remote and incredibly isolated community based out of Village Bay on Hirta. Due to the extreme environment they called home, the people of St Kilda evolved a unique style of island life, almost entirely self-sufficient and scarcely touched by the outside world.

For thousands of years the islanders of St Kilda carved a life out of the land and the resources they had available. You would imagine this to involve fishing their plentiful coastline, however the waters here are often treacherous and the weather too inconsistent to rely on. A resource St Kilda does have in abundance are seabirds, the islander's biggest commodity. Using home-made ropes, islanders would climb and abseil barefoot on the 400-metre-high cliffs of Hirta, as well as the surrounding islands and sea stacks, to collect birds. The meat could be dried and stored for winter, the eggs could be eaten in summer, the oil from the birds used to fuel lamps, the skin turned into shoes, and the feathers used for clothing and bed-stuffing. As the rest of the world built vast economies, fought wars and strove to build their perfect form of societies, an ancient and sustainable way of life was preserved on Hirta. This was until 29 August 1930, when the 36 remaining islanders voted to leave their island home. Numbers were dwindling, sickness was spreading and finally life here became unsustainable.

We spent a glorious day in the Atlantic sunshine exploring the island of Hirta by foot. Before leaving this historic land, we had to enter its alluring clear blue waters for a swim. At low tide, swimming from Village Bay's sandy beach straight into the shallow waters of the bay is a great option. As we were here at high tide, we opted to swim from the small jetty to the left of the main village. The water here is deep, cold and a brilliant clear blue. Looking back onto Village Bay and the smooth, steep hills of Hirta from the water was the perfect way to end our trip to the true Atlantis of the Atlantic.

A trip to this isolated and remote archipelago is a truly life-changing experience and the opportunity to swim in its water was a real privilege. St Kilda is a Scottish blue space like no other. It is so much more than a venue to visit for a swim or other watersports. The islands' habitats, weather, history and vistas are so deeply woven into their surrounding blue space, the magnificent North Atlantic Ocean, which continuously laps at St Kilda's shores.

THE NORTH

ACHMELVICH BAY

Activities	Swimming, paddleboarding, kayaking
Experience level	＊ ＊
Environment	Ocean
Start point	Achmelvich Bay car park
Carry time	5 mins
Public transport	Bus connections from Ullapool
OS map	442

Achmelvich is a real gem on the north-west coast of Scotland. Here you will find two white sandy beaches, clear blue water, and many hidden coves and caves dotted around the bay. Achmelvich is a brilliant blue space to explore and well worth the detour off the main North Coast 500 route for a swim, paddleboard or kayak.

Access to Achmelvich Bay is down a slightly precarious single-track road, so do take care here; it can get busy on a warm summer's day. Don't let this deter you, though. The toil of the road is completely worth it, as at the end of the track you will find a small slice of Scottish paradise.

Achmelvich is a huge crescent-shaped bay, broken up by granite outcrops and accompanied by the stunning backdrop of the epic mountains of

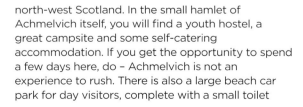

north-west Scotland. In the small hamlet of Achmelvich itself, you will find a youth hostel, a great campsite and some self-catering accommodation. If you get the opportunity to spend a few days here, do – Achmelvich is not an experience to rush. There is also a large beach car park for day visitors, complete with a small toilet block, a tap for refilling water bottles or rinsing wetsuits, and some rubbish disposal bins.

The first sandy bay that you come to at Achmelvich is by far the most popular and it is easy to see why. This beach looks like a postcard from a Caribbean island: glorious white sand, with enticing clear water lapping at its shores. This main beach faces north-west and has some protection granted by the rocky outcrop of An Fharaid Bheag, making it a great beginner-friendly or family blue space for swimmers and other water users.

We had spotted a second cove on the map and decided to walk to it on the hunt for a more secluded swim. We took the steep path up from the beach, heading north, and traversed the headland, dodging sheep and watching black-and-white guillemots bobbing on the water until we caught sight of the second cove of Achmelvich. Facing west, it is slightly more exposed to the ocean swell: as we watched from the cliff top, big waves rolled in and dumped onto the shore. The two dog walkers on the beach soon left and we had this sandy paradise to ourselves. We got into our wetsuits and

swam in the clear waters of Achmelvich Bay, doing laps of the shore to warm up and bobbing about in the swell like the guillemots.

If you are interested in a little more adventure, Achmelvich Bay is a brilliant place to explore on a paddleboard or in a kayak. You just have to scan an OS map to see the number of hidden coves within the bay; all would make a brilliant short journey in favourable conditions. Just south of Achmelvich and around the headland, you will find Loch Roe, an intricate sea loch with a seal colony, many islands and a shipwreck that reveals itself as the tide drops.

Achmelvich Bay is a superb slice of blue health and a place to slow down, recharge and absorb its beauty.

SCOURIE BAY

Activities	Paddleboarding, swimming, kayaking
Experience level	✱ ✱
Environment	Ocean
Start point	Scourie Bay beach
Carry time	Beachside parking
Public transport	N/A
OS map	445

On the far north-west coast of Scotland lies the remote and sheltered blue space of Scourie Bay. Here you will find golden sand, clear waters and a real sanctuary for swimming, paddleboarding and kayaking, protected from the often-turbulent North Atlantic Ocean.

The crofting village of Scourie provides a welcome rest stop on the road north from Ullapool. It is a great spot to slow the pace and relax for a night or two. As you drive into Scourie itself, there is a large golden beach on your left-hand side, overlooked by a well-equipped hilltop campsite. In the village itself you will find a petrol station,

a post office, and a handful of hotels and guest houses to choose from.

We arrived late one summer's afternoon and got a last-minute pitch for our campervan. The campsite is on terraced levels, giving almost every pitch an exceptional view out over Scourie Bay. A young harbour seal bobbed about in the bay to the great amusement of many. It was an hour before sunset when I finally pumped up my board and headed down to the water, the golden evening light just beginning to illuminate the water's surface.

There are two main options for getting onto

the water at Scourie Bay: the sandy stretch on the southern side of the bay, or on the east side there is a rocky beach stretched out in front of the pier. I got on the water from the rocky beach, for the simple reason that it was closer to the camping pitch, and I'm not one to carry my board further than is required!

From the shelter of the bay, I could see huge Atlantic waves out to sea; they would rise on the horizon and crash down against the rocks just outside the bay. However, inside the bay the water was relatively calm, with just a gentle rocking motion from the swell. I looked to the campsite above me and realised that the seal must have gone on its way because I was now the evening entertainment for the 50 or so people enjoying a drink outside their tents and motorhomes. I even saw one chap get out the long lens of his camera to track me on the water . . . As strange as this was, nothing could lessen my enjoyment of this paddle. A solo sunset paddle from the safety of a sheltered

bay as the Atlantic Ocean roared just outside: there is no better way to absorb the blue-health benefits this country has to offer.

If you are interested in more of the adventure that Scourie Bay has to offer, there is a great kayaking journey outside the bay. Handa Island lies just north of Scourie Bay and it is a 10-mile round trip to circumnavigate the island via Tarbet by sea kayak. Handa Island is a Site of Special Scientific Interest as well as a nature reserve, home to 200,000 seabirds nestled along its cliffs. With sea stacks and caves to explore, as well as stunning views towards Cape Wrath, this is a truly awesome adventure. If you would like to visit Handa Island but don't fancy the paddle, there is a small ferry that runs a service during the summer months from Tarbet.

The shelter of Scourie Bay makes it a great blue space for swimmers and beginner paddlers, as well as those wanting a relaxed sunset paddle before a pint and chips at the campsite pub.

DURNESS

Activities	Swimming, paddleboarding, kayaking, surfing
Experience level	✳ ✳
Environment	Ocean
Start point	Various locations
Carry time	Less than 5 minutes
Public transport	Bus services from Inverness
OS map	446

Durness is the most north-westerly village on the British mainland, and it's where the seemingly never-ending north coast road finally turns south. When approaching Durness from the east, rolling farmland soon turns to the towering cliffs and rugged mountains that we associate with the west coast of Scotland. On the doorstep of this beautiful village are a magnitude of incredible blue spaces to explore, including many white sandy beaches and hidden coves, with cliff-top walks and incredible wildlife flocking to this abundant habitat. Along this small stretch of coastline, you will find beaches facing west and north-east, giving you a pick of locations for watersports, depending on which way the wind is blowing.

Durness itself is one of the most traveller-friendly villages you will come across on a tour of the far north of Scotland. Here you will find plenty of accommodation options, including a stunningly situated campsite, petrol station, shops, a tourist information centre and, most importantly, a pub. Less than a mile to the east lies one of the north coast's biggest tourist attractions, Smoo Cave. Carved out of limestone cliffs, this dramatic sea cave

boasts a huge 50-foot cavernous entrance, leading to a hidden underground network. Geological tours of the cave are available throughout the main season which incorporate a short subterranean boat journey through the cave network – worth a trip if you are interested in exploring underground blue spaces too.

Along the coastline of Durness, you have your pick of stunning beaches. The closest to the village is the north-east-facing Sango Bay, just a five-minute walk away. The Sango Sands campsite looms above the beach from the cliff top, with excellent views from every pitch. The beach is made up of sprawling white sand, interspersed with jagged rock stacks protruding out of the sand and sea. The water here is crystal clear, and incredibly enticing for a swim even with gentle waves peeling along its shoreline. On a calm day it would be brilliant to paddleboard or kayak between these jagged rock stacks close to high tide. Due to its accessibility, this is one of the most popular beaches in the area, but in the far reaches of Scotland there's very little risk of overcrowding.

Three miles to the east of Durness you will find Ceannabeinne Beach, another stunning north-east-facing beach overlooking the low-lying island of Eilean Hoan. This uninterrupted stretch of pale sand is backed by steep cliffs and topped with craggy outcrops. It's stunning to dip below its clear blue surface, or to enjoy it from above on a paddleboard or kayak trip, if the conditions allow.

For people who like their blue spaces mixed with adrenaline, the Golden Eagle zip line crosses part of the beach here at Ceannabeinne. This is the most northerly zip line in western Europe, where you can jump from the top of a 38-metre cliff and fly across the beach.

One mile to the west of Durness village lies a huge, wild stretch of sand called Balnakeil. This sweeping crescent-shaped beach covers much of the west flank of the rocky Faraid Head. It differs from the other beaches of Durness by the fact it faces due west, meaning that if conditions aren't right for entering the other blue spaces close by, they may be very different here. As you approach the beach, you will find a small parking area backed by the imposing Balnakeil House, built in the eighteenth century as a home for the local laird but now a rental holiday home. Directly in front of you is the abandoned seventeenth-century church and graveyard watching over the bay.

The village of Durness and its surrounding coastline are a wonder to explore. Take your time here, slow the pace a little and soak up all that this far north-west tip of Scotland has to offer.

STRATHY BAY

Activities	Surfing, swimming, paddleboarding, kayaking
Experience level	✳ ✳ ✳ ✳
Environment	Ocean
Start point	Car park next to graveyard
Carry time	5 minutes
Public transport	Bus connections from Thurso
OS map	449

Located 20 miles west of the town of Thurso along the north coast of Scotland is the remote and wild blue space of Strathy Bay. It's a large, golden sandy beach backed by crumbling dunes and fed to the west by the peaty waters of the River Strathy. Strathy Bay is a space to sit and absorb this untamed, rugged coastline and, if you are skilled enough, enter the turbulent waters of one of the north coast's premier surf destinations.

To the west of the bay, Strathy Point headland extends far into the ocean, culminating with Strathy Point lighthouse at its tip; the lighthouse has been warning ships to stay away from these rocky shores since the mid-twentieth century. If your schedule allows, I would highly recommend walking down to the lighthouse. It takes about 25 minutes from the

small car park on the edge of Strathy Point and when you finally reach the lighthouse you are rewarded with stunning 360-degree views. It's the perfect position for spotting the wildlife that calls Scotland's north coast home.

However, to reach our blue space at Strathy Bay, access is a little easier. The main beach car park is signposted off the A836. Take this turning and follow the track ahead as it winds through some small hills and past a cemetery, then you will see the car park and a log cabin in front of you. The log cabin at Strathy Bay is a brilliant example of community activism to protect the natural environment. During the late 1990s a local group was established here to help protect this area. They are named the Strathy Bay Environmental Action

Group (SBEAG) and they raised funds for the building of the log cabin, which now houses a toilet for visitors to the beach and cemetery, as well as information boards, useful tools for teaching visitors about the local environment and the importance of protecting it.

It is no wonder that local residents work so tirelessly to protect Strathy Bay. This short stretch of coastline incorporating Strathy Point and Bay, Armadale and Melvich has been recognised as a Site of Special Scientific Interest (SSSI). This area is home to many rare coastal plants and flowers, including the *Primula Scotica*, known as the Scottish primrose, which flowers above the beach in late May and early June, as well as the honey-scented frog orchid. For the twitchers among us, there are plenty of brilliant seabirds to be seen from Strathy Bay, including plump puffins, orange-beaked oystercatchers and the miniature ringed plovers.

Strathy Bay is a Blue Flag beach, meaning it has been recognised for its pristine local environment and water quality. However, when you look out over the river mouth as the tide retreats you will see brown water draining into the bay and turning the white sea foam a dirty-looking colour. This is simply the effect of water travelling through peaty ground further upstream, staining the water. Do not fear: this water is perfectly safe to swim or surf in.

In terms of surfing, one of the main breaks at Strathy is in this peaty brown river mouth, where left and right peaks are surfable on a higher tide. There are also a variety of breaks along the sandbar the whole length of Strathy Bay, surfable on all tides. When the swell isn't surging in from the North Atlantic and the wind has been tamed, Strathy Bay can be a great place to explore by kayak and paddleboard or to take a swim in its icy water.

Strathy Bay has a wild and remote feel, and is protected by environmentally focused local residents so that wildlife can thrive and visitors can soak up this stunning blue space for many years to come. It is a must-visit beach for the whole family, and if conditions and your skillset allows, there is plenty of adventure to be had in the water.

THURSO EAST

Activities	Surfing
Experience level	★ ★ ★ ★ ★
Environment	Ocean
Start point	Car park opposite break
Carry time	5 minutes
Public transport	Train station in Thurso
OS map	451

Located on Scotland's frigid north shore, 20 miles west of John o' Groats, is world-renowned surf spot Thurso East. It's a spectacular reef, found a stone's throw from the shore of the UK mainland's most northerly town, Thurso. Despite the remote location, this mesmerising reef break attracts surfers from all over the world. Once a year it is home to the Scottish National Surfing Championships, when the best surfers in Scotland compete for the national shortboard and longboard titles.

Thurso is an unassuming town. It sits at 59° north, which is in fact the same latitude as the capital of Alaska, Juneau. Its name is a reminiscence of its significant Norse heritage: under Viking rule, it acted as a pivotal port linking Scotland to Europe. When you arrive into Thurso's grey pebble-dashed residential streets, it is hard to believe that this northerly outpost is a mecca for surfers worldwide. The majority of the local community take no interest in the surf scene here. Yet hundreds of surfers make the pilgrimage each year to the far tip of Scotland to seek out the reef at Thurso East.

The key to its notoriety lies under the surface. This iconic spot has some unique underwater topography. The wave at Thurso East breaks onto a kelp-covered slab-stone reef, located next to the mouth of the River Thurso. Here the raw power of North Atlantic swell is shaped by the reef into picture-perfect right-hand waves. When the swell rolls in from a northerly direction, the wave tends to wall up, creating towering clean faces. But when the swell direction swings more from the west, Thurso East can conjure up deep, hollow barrelling waves up to 100 metres in length.

Thurso East is best surfed on a mid-rising tide, when the wind is blowing offshore from the southeast. The main surf season runs between October and April, when big North Atlantic swells roll in from the Arctic. The cold water here is exacerbated by the icy flow from the River Thurso flowing out into the bay. If you are considering surfing this wave during the main swell season, a thick wetsuit, gloves, boots and a hood are vital.

Rachel and I arrived on the north coast in early October, eager and excited to see Thurso East working in all its glory. We headed straight down to the spot where Google Maps told us the wave was, driving through a gathering of old farm buildings and into a large farmyard overlooking the ocean with the uneasy feeling that we were trespassing on

someone's property. There was not a soul in sight and only the smallest ripple on the water gently caressing the shoreline. We were convinced we were in the wrong location until we noticed a piece of farm equipment covered in surf stickers, the only indication of this place's epic surf heritage on a waveless day.

We returned the next day to a buzzing car park full of neoprene-clad surfers, with accents from every corner of the British Isles. Looking out onto the bay, it was a different ocean to the millpond from the day before. Beautifully formed head-high waves peeled along the reef in front of our eyes. We watched a set of six or seven perfectly formed waves, a surfer dropping into each, then the long lull while the surfers used the rip from the river mouth to get back out behind the waves, then another set,

with even more skill on show. To enter the water at Thurso East you need to be a very competent surfer, with experience in these types of conditions. On this day Rachel and I were more than happy to watch the action and take photos from the safety of the shore. On the far skyline to the east, we spotted the towering cliffs of Orkney rising out of the ocean, generously adding to the dramatics of this epic blue space.

The wave at Thurso East is one of the great wonders of Scotland – to be held on a pedestal and honoured by surfers and non-surfers alike. It is an ambition of mine to one day surf here, but blue spaces don't always have to be entered to reap the benefits. On this day, I got so much from simply watching this blue space going off in all its glory.

DUNNET BEACH

Activities	Surfing, paddleboarding, kayaking, swimming
Experience level	✳ ✳ ✳
Environment	Ocean
Start point	Car park next to caravan park
Carry time	5 minutes
Public transport	Bus connections from Thurso
OS map	451

Lying just 7 miles to the east of the town of Thurso on Scotland's rugged north coast are the sprawling sands of Dunnet Beach. This sweeping crescent-shaped bay extends for 2 miles from the settlement of Castletown to the towering cliffs of Dunnet Head. Tall, machair-covered sand dunes separate the beach from the main A836 north coast road, giving this windswept bay a remote and wild feel. Dunnet Beach is a brilliant blue space for surfing; the waves are much more forgiving than their neighbours at

Thurso East. When the conditions allow, Dunnet Beach can be an incredible space to explore via kayak or paddleboard; you can launch from either end of the beach and have the freedom to explore the whole bay and flanking headlands.

Dunnet Beach's human history dates back to the early Bronze Age, with archaeological excavations unearthing hut circles located close to Dunnet forest from 2500 BC. Fast forward 3,500 years and Dunnet Bay became an important Norse

settlement in the tenth century AD. These settlers were farmers, not Viking warriors, whose ambition was to etch a life out of the lands of Caithness, growing crops and fishing in the waters around Dunnet Beach.

To access the beach, there is a large car park situated next to the caravan and camping site at the most north-easterly end of the bay. Here you will find plenty of space for parking, various boards with information on exploring the area's exciting Viking history, and a wooden walkway down to the open sands. Other options for parking include a small car park nestled in the dunes halfway along the beach and another small car park at the Castletown end of the bay.

Dunnet Head flanks the north edge of the bay, its sheer cliffs stretching out into the ocean making it the UK mainland's most northerly point. Here you will find a 66-foot-tall lighthouse and much information about local wildlife you could be lucky enough to spot from this vantage point. Non-human visitors to the bay include seals, dolphins and the occasional whale, along with a whole host of spectacular seabirds who nest on the steep cliffs of Dunnet Head. A walk along this headland is a must for any visitors to Caithness. On a clear day, the views out over to Orkney are simply sensational.

Dunnet Beach offers a more beginner-friendly beach break for surfing than many of the other north coast beaches. The bay faces north-west and picks up a large amount of North Atlantic swell. On a good day, long peeling waves break the whole way along the shoreline. However, on larger days do be conscious of strong rip currents along the length of the beach, as well as sharp rocks when the tide drops out. Dunnet Beach is home to the North Coast

Watersports Surf School, a local company run by a lovely, passionate couple, Iona and Finn, who have both held Scottish surf titles at one point in their lives. Check them out for surf lessons and equipment hire.

This is a glorious, never-ending stretch of sand offering something a little different to other beaches on this coastline. Make sure to visit to soak up this rugged blue space on the tip of Britain from in and out of the water.

WHALIGOE STEPS

Activities	Swimming
Experience level	✳ ✳
Environment	Ocean
Start point	Car park next to cottages
Carry time	15 minutes to water's edge
Public transport	Bus connections from Wick
OS map	450

The Whaligoe Steps are situated on Scotland's far north-eastern coastline and are a dramatic access point to an even more dramatic blue space. Here you will find a staircase of 330 steps carved into the sheer cliff face, descending into a large natural harbour. The harbour is surrounded on three sides by 250-foot-tall overhanging sea cliffs, and on the remaining side it lies open to the turbulent North Sea. In the right conditions, a dip into this blue space can be a truly exhilarating experience.

Located just 7 miles south of Wick, the Whaligoe Steps are slowly becoming a tourist attraction along this stretch of remote coastline. There is a small parking area past a row of cottages just off the A99

road. At present there is only enough space for about five cars, so do park with consideration and be prepared to wait for people to return to their cars and free up a space for you. From the car park, follow the small path towards the ocean past a large house until you emerge at the top of the staircase. When we visited, the steps were in the process of being restored by a local stonemason. The new steps are wide and feel relatively safe; however, I would still recommend sturdy shoes and a good head for heights.

As we descended, we watched huge rolling waves crash onto the cliffs just outside the harbour. Seafoam would be flung into the air and instantly caught by the wind, which jettisoned it high into the sky. As the airborne white foam got caught in the sunlight it looked like seabirds circling the sky above us.

These incredible steps date back to the mid-eighteenth century and the boom in herring fishing off the east coast. At this time, herring was considered a delicacy on the Continent and in relative abundance in Scottish waters. At its peak, the harbour at Whaligoe would have had more than 20 boats working from it. The use of this natural harbour gradually declined into the twentieth century until the last boat ceased fishing from Whaligoe in the 1960s.

As you reach the bottom of the steps, you will see a large grassy area known as The Bink, which was used for landing and sorting fish. Further to the right, under the overhanging cliff, is a small pebbled beach sloping down to the water's edge. We headed here for our swim, walking past old winches and chains rusted by time spent so close to the ocean; it was interesting to see the remains of this busy blue space's history. From deep within this inlet the effect

of this natural harbour is impressive. Out on the horizon you can see the white horses galloping on the water's surface, but in the shelter of the inner harbour the water was calm and inviting. After a quick dip in the ocean, we retraced our steps up the staircase, lugging our damp wetsuits but feeling exhilarated from this historic dip.

Walking down the steps, you almost feel like you are walking off the edge of the world. The true force of the ocean is laid out in front of you. The Whaligoe Steps are a must-visit if you are in the area, for a swim or to simply soak up the blue health benefits of this location via the precarious descent route.

LOCH NESS

Activities	Paddleboarding, kayaking, swimming
Experience level	✱ ✱
Environment	Freshwater loch
Start point	Layby at Inchnacardoch Bay
Carry time	Lochside parking
Public transport	Bus connections from Inverness and Fort William
OS map	416

When people across the globe think of Scotland, they often consider Loch Ness and the legend of a large monster living below its dark surface. This vast expanse of water is on every visitor's bucket list, each of them hoping to get a glimpse of Nessie. As a blue space, Loch Ness is on another level to many other Scottish lochs: it is vast and awe-inspiring, and because of this it's easy to find tranquillity away from the hype.

My favourite fact about Loch Ness is that, by volume, it holds more water than all the lakes in England and Wales put together: 7,452 million cubic

metres of water, to be exact. Loch Ness extends from the town of Fort Augustus for 23 miles towards the Highland capital of Inverness and is a large section of the Caledonian Canal. Constructed in the early nineteenth century, the system of intricate canals, locks and vast lochs links the west coast town of Fort William to the east coast in Inverness, running through the Great Glen fault line, formed at the end of the last Ice Age. This slash across the country can even be seen from space!

If you are up for a big paddling adventure, the Great Glen Challenge takes place every year. Paddlers race across this 57-mile stretch in either one or two days, a massive undertaking but an epic achievement.

There are an infinite number of places to paddle and swim along the north and south shores of Loch Ness. Due to its vastness, even a small amount of wind can have an impact on the water's surface; on a rough day, large wind-generated waves can even appear on the surface! However, on a calm day the views of the surrounding mountains from the water are simply stunning.

With a moderate wind blowing in from the west on the day we visited Loch Ness, we opted to head to sheltered Inchnacardoch Bay. Located on the loch's north shore, not far along the A82 from Fort Augustus, this natural bay is a relatively sheltered area when the prevailing westerly wind blows across the main body of the loch.

At Inchnacardoch Bay you will find a large layby on the loch side of the road, big enough for five or six cars and a small sunken slipway leading directly onto the water. In the bay itself there are several eerie-looking shipwrecks with peeling paint, rusty metal and hulls riddled with holes. As a person passionate about preserving the natural world, I should view these abandoned boats in their simplest form as large pollutants of this beautiful blue space, but I can't help but be intrigued by them. There is something strangely alluring about a shipwreck. I wonder about the story each one has to tell, of where it sailed and who had been aboard it during its life.

After checking out the shipwrecks it was time to head towards Inchnacardoch Bay's biggest paddling attraction. Cherry Island is less than a couple of hundred metres from the slipway and is easy to circumnavigate in a few minutes. As I paddled out towards the island, I could see the wind whipping up the water's surface on the main body of the loch; we'd made the right decision to paddle in this bay! After a quick scan along the horizon for Nessie, I paddled back to shore, happy with this small and easy-to-access blue journey.

Loch Ness has endless possibilities for big or small adventures, however you would like to tailor them. It is a bucket-list tick for many visitors to Scotland, but a great playground for locals too.

THE NORTH-EAST

BOW FIDDLE ROCK

Activities	Swimming, paddleboarding, kayaking
Experience level	✳ ✳ ✳
Environment	Ocean
Start point	Addison Street, Portknockie
Carry time	10 minutes
Public transport	Bus connections from Portknockie
OS map	425

Situated off the headland at Portknockie on the Moray coast is Bow Fiddle Rock, an awe-inspiring natural sea arch carved out of Cullen quartzite rock by the artistic hand of the North Sea. In the right conditions, Bow Fiddle Rock is a spectacular venue for wild swimming, paddleboarding and kayaking, but even when conditions are less favourable it is an incredible landmark to be viewed from the safety of the coastal path.

Bow Fiddle Rock is named after its resemblance to the tip of a fiddle bow, but to me it looks more like an inviting gateway to the north. This mesmerizing sea arch had been at the top of my list

of places to visit during our *Blue Scotland* project and when we finally reached the Moray coast in early October we were blessed with calm seas and light winds. We met with a local friend soon after sunrise for a swim out to thread the eye of the needle of this impressive natural sculpture.

Arrival at Bow Fiddle Rock is not what you might expect at one of Scotland's most photographed locations. Parking is available on the edge of a residential estate on Addison Street – but do park here with care and respect for local residents. Bow Fiddle Rock was their backyard long before it rose to Instagram fame. From Addison Street, you can

follow an obvious path down to a colourful bench overlooking the small cove where the archway resides. The rock is beautifully framed on both sides by the steep cliffs of the bay. From the bench, turn left down the path for a few metres until you spot a steep descent to the cove: take care here, as there is a lot of loose rock. At the head of the cove is a grassy expanse that quickly turns to a pebbled beach as you stroll down to the water's edge.

The sea arch lies about 100 metres from the shore. It isn't much of a distance for a strong swimmer, but the difficulty comes with any swell or wind and strong tides. The best time to swim here is as the tide is rising to high water; there will be less movement in the tidal system and the cove will be full of water. There are many submerged rocks in the bay to avoid if you are paddleboarding or kayaking, but they do make great rest stops for swimmers.

Floating in the water and looking up at the main

structure of this sea arch is a dizzying experience. From close up, the arch looks more fragile than from afar. You can't help but have thoughts of it crumbling on top of you – until you remind yourself that it has stood firm against the force of the North Sea for thousands of years.

Much of this beautiful structure lies hidden beneath the water's surface, and with Rachel's underwater camera we could see the continuation of the arch stretching to the seabed. Around the back of the rock we found seagulls and shags drying off their wings in the sun after an early morning fishing trip. These birds had the right idea – the water was icy, and soon the cold began to seep through our wetsuits, so we headed back to the shore. Bow Fiddle Rock had exceeded even my high expectations of this epic blue space.

This alluring natural sculpture emerging from the North Sea is an incredible sight to witness from land and, even better, from the water.

SANDEND BAY

Activities	Surfing, swimming, kayaking, paddleboarding
Experience level	✱ ✱
Environment	Ocean
Start point	Beach car park
Carry time	Less than 5 minutes
Public transport	Bus connections from Aberdeen
OS map	425

Sandend Bay is a jewel on Scotland's Moray coast. Here you will find sand dunes backing a large north-facing golden beach which slopes gently into the water. Overlooking the beach is the picturesque village of Sandend, made up of a handful of quaint colourful cottages and a small working harbour. This beach often picks up North Sea swell and is a popular spot for surfers, as well as swimmers, kayakers and families on warm summer days.

Sandend is sandwiched between the Moray towns of Cullen to the west and Portsoy to the east. The beach is accessed down a narrow road off the main A98 coastal route. You will soon reach a large campsite and caravan park on your right-hand side; next door to this is a small beach car park and public toilets. This is the extent of the tourist facilities at Sandend, which adds to the wild feel of this beach, but do make sure to take a packed lunch with you!

Rachel and I arrived at Sandend in early October and got a great pitch on the beachfront of the

campsite, having missed the main summer rush. The campsite has basic but good facilities, and nothing can beat waking up to the sound of waves breaking on the shore. We pumped up our paddleboards and headed down to the water, our intention being to paddle west up the coast for about a mile to Findlater Castle – or the ruins of the castle, I should say. These stand on a rocky peninsula that juts out into the sea some 50 feet above the water. However, as we got onto the water the wind picked up much more than had been forecast, so we decided to play it safe and stay within Sandend Bay itself. We explored the small fishing harbour, met the locals (two inquisitive seals) and played in the swell, attempting to surf on our paddleboards until the sun began to set.

Sandend Bay is a popular surfing destination and has fairly consistent surf, with peaks along the length of the beach. Sandend is best surfed on a lower tide. Due to its northerly aspect, the best swell direction

comes from the north or north-east, and an offshore wind will blow from the south. Unfortunately for us, during our visit the swell never materialised, but Sandend is on my list to return to when next in Scotland's North-east.

We may not have had the surf at Sandend, but on our last evening we were treated to an even rarer phenomenon when the Aurora Borealis lit up the sky over the village. If it weren't for Rachel's keen photographer's eye, I would have completely missed it. To our naked eyes, it looked like a dancing white cloud on the horizon, but the long exposure on the camera showed us this dynamic light display in all its glory. It was my first time seeing the northern lights in Scotland and an incredible way to end our trip to this lovely seaside village.

Sandend Bay is off the beaten track and a great place to escape to for a few days of soaking up the ocean, surfing, swimming, paddleboarding or Aurora hunting.

HELL'S LUM, CULLYKHAN BAY

Activities	Swimming, paddleboarding, kayaking
Experience level	✳ ✳
Environment	Ocean
Start point	Car parks at Cullykhan Bay
Carry time	15 minutes
Public transport	Bus connections from Fraserburgh
OS map	426

Equidistant between the seaside towns of Fraserburgh and Banff, Hell's Lum, near Cullykhan beach, is a network of hidden caves, quiet bays and secluded swimming pools carved out of the sea cliffs by the power of the North Sea. Hell's Lum and its adjacent coastline are a brilliant venue for a chilly dip or an explorative paddleboard or kayak journey.

There is a large car park just off of the main B9031 coastal road which is signposted for Cullykhan beach. The views out over the North Sea from the car park itself are stunning. From here, you have the choice to either turn right down to Cullykhan Bay itself or left down to the sea pools of Hell's Lum. Cullykhan Bay is a large, sandy beach

sheltered from the prevailing winds by tall sea cliffs. It is accessed down an obvious stepped path and boardwalk. The beach itself is a brilliant place to swim or to launch paddleboards or kayaks; from here, you can explore the bay, find hidden sea caves and even venture around the headland.

We decided to turn left out of the car park in search of Hell's Lum and its cave network and secluded natural swimming pools. There is a faint path running alongside a fence that we followed until we reached a gap in the fence and an obvious path descending the cliffs on the other side. Do take care on this path; it is incredibly steep, with huge drops looming in front of you. From this precarious

path, you will get your first views of Hell's Lum, a partially collapsed sea cave whose large gaping black mouth has opened on the opposite cliff. From this visible mouth of Hell's Lum, sea caves extend into the cliffs and emerge again down at the water's edge, creating a hidden passageway deep in the hillside. We visited in relatively calm weather, but I have been told that when the North Sea is firing, white frothy sea foam bursts out of the mouth of Hell's Lum – an incredible spectacle, I am sure.

Once down at sea level we carefully scrambled across the wet, slippery rocks to reach the sheltered pools near the water's edge. Here we found a whole network of them, extending from the cave and

opening out into the North Sea. In a moment of trust, Rachel thrust her camera at me and excitedly jumped into the pool for a refreshing afternoon dip. The pools are relatively sheltered from the prevailing westerly wind and would be a great place to spend time on a warm summer's day. As the swell gently flowed in and out of the pools, you could hear it eerily crashing and echoing deep within the cave system up to the expectant mouth of Hell's Lum.

The pools at Hell's Lum offer a beautiful and relatively sheltered place to take a dip in the North Sea. Here you will find ample amounts of adventure, exploring nearby Cullykhan Bay and its surrounding coastline.

ABERDEEN CITY BEACH

Activities	Surfing, swimming, paddleboarding, kayaking
Experience level	✳
Environment	Ocean
Start point	Beach promenade
Carry time	Less than 5 minutes
Public transport	Various bus links from city centre
OS map	406

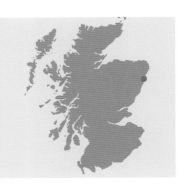

Scotland's third-largest city lies on the chilly north-east coast of Scotland and has its very own blue space. The sprawling sands of Aberdeen city beach extend 2 miles from the mouth of the River Dee in the south to the mouth of the River Don in the north. Aberdeen is often nicknamed the Granite City due to its stone architecture – its buildings sparkle like the ocean when the sun shines on them. However, when the sun isn't shining, as often happens in Scotland, Aberdeen adopts an industrial feel, its sprawling shipyards and reputation as the oil and gas capital of Europe thankfully softened by this blue space on its doorstep. Aberdeen has a vibrant surf community, alongside year-round hardy wild swimmers, and a host of kayakers and paddleboarders who share a love for this harsh but rewarding coastline.

The sands of Aberdeen city beach are interspersed by regular wooden groynes jutting out from the beach into the breaking waves. This

infrastructure has been put in place to reduce coastal erosion; however, care needs to be taken when entering any blue space with this type of infrastructure: there is an increased risk of rip currents running along the groynes and a potential for leash entanglement in the structure.

Aberdeen city beach is backed by a high sea wall, and on top a promenade which runs the length of the beach, popular with walkers and cyclists on sunny summer days. The promenade is also a bit of a commercial hub, with various chain restaurants, independent cafes, shops and even an indoor and outdoor theme park just a stone's throw from the ocean. Out to sea, large wind turbines gently spin on the horizon.

The surf scene in Aberdeen began slowly in the 1960s, with a handful of hardy locals heading out into the waves on handmade boards. Over the decades it has grown considerably. The city is home to two universities with surf clubs and when the waves are good you will see surfers out enjoying this blue space. There are two main surf areas at Aberdeen city beach, one at the most southerly end near the harbour wall and the other at the beach's most northerly end near the mouth of the River Don.

The spot to the south is well known for its reef next to the harbour wall and it works well on a large southerly swell; a strong rip runs out next to the harbour wall when the swell is big. Further along this southerly section of beach there is a sandbar that provides a more mellow wave, even with the smallest swell. This area is best surfed on a lower tide to avoid any backwash from the harbour wall.

The surf spot to the north of Aberdeen city beach works better on a higher tide. On larger swell days, do watch out for rip currents caused by the groynes; there have been incidents of surfers getting swept over them and, as previously mentioned, the potential for leash entanglement is high.

Looking north of the River Don, the coastline quickly becomes less industrial, giving way to large sandy stretches, extensive wildlife and quieter waves. Balmedie beach, to the north of Aberdeen, has a long, sandy shoreline backed by dunes and nature trails, a brilliant place for swimming and paddleboarding on a calm day, or, when the wind is blowing, this stretch of coastline north of the city becomes a kite surfer's haven.

Having this stretch of beach on the doorstep of this industrial city is a huge asset for locals and visitors alike; the opportunity to soak up the benefits of the ocean from the water or the promenade can't be undervalued.

STONEHAVEN AND DUNNOTTAR CASTLE

Activities	Surfing, swimming, paddleboarding, kayaking
Experience level	★ ★ ★ ★
Environment	Ocean
Start point	Shorehead Road
Carry time	5 minutes
Public transport	Train station in Stonehaven
OS map	396

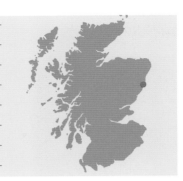

Nestled along the Aberdeenshire coastline, 16 miles south of the city itself, is Stonehaven. A picturesque harbour town with a large, sandy seafront and plenty of great facilities, it is an incredible blue space to explore, with its clear waters, sheltered bays and truly epic coastline extending north and south.

Stonehaven beach itself is a long, sandy stretch exposed to the North Sea. This beach can be a great surfing destination on a south-easterly or north-easterly swell, with the offshore wind coming from the west. On the southern corner you will also find a good quality right-hander reef break to enjoy. During the summer months the swell here is much less consistent, providing paddleboarding and swimming possibilities from the beach itself.

If you are looking for a more sheltered location to swim or paddleboard, you can head around to the harbour. There is a quaint wee beach which is protected by Downie Point headland to the right and the south pier to the left, making it a brilliant spot for beginners to practise their paddling. This beach is also home to Stonehaven Paddle Boarding, a local company offering SUP lessons, tours and rentals.

Due to the recent increase in paddleboarding in this area, Aberdeen Council has published guidelines

to ensure the safety of those using the water. Paddleboarding is permitted in the Botany Bay area of the harbour, between the south pier and southern coastline. However, it is not permitted within the harbour walls themselves or the navigational channel, where boats come in and out. Anyone paddling north needs to give the harbour a wide berth and your passage south must keep in close to the cliffs.

Rachel and I met early one summer's morning to paddle from Stonehaven harbour down to the famous Dunnottar Castle, a ruined fortress perched on the cliff edge about 2 miles to the south. We

managed to park on Shorehead Road, next to the harbour. Feeling too guilty to switch on the noisy electric pump, as people slept in the nearby cottages, we pumped up the boards by hand, getting a good warm-up for our paddle adventure. We found a handy slipway down to the water's edge and were soon on the glassy water of Botany Bay, gliding over the kelp beds.

After rounding the first headland of Downie Point, we found some amazing sea caves and hidden nooks that you can paddle directly into. For most, we also needed to reverse out of them or they involved an impractical 20-point turn. From

here we paddled across Strathlethan Bay and past Dunnicaer sea stack, where hundreds of seabirds rest on the cliffs. This stretch of coastline is a haven for all types of seabird. Just south of here is RSPB Fowlsheugh Nature Reserve, home to more than 100,000 breeding seabirds. Along this coast you will find guillemots, razorbills, kittiwakes, puffins and fulmars.

After rounding Bowdun Head, we arrived in a bay aptly named Castle Haven, where the mighty Dunnottar Castle perches on the opposite cliff top. Dunnottar has played a pivotal role in Scotland's history throughout the centuries, most famously being the location where the Scottish crown jewels were hidden from Oliver Cromwell's invading army in the seventeenth century and as a strategic defensive location in the eighteenth-century Jacobite Rising. The castle is a world-renowned tourist attraction, with thousands of visitors each year, but for me nothing beats experiencing Scotland's epic history from the water.

The Stonehaven to Dunnottar Castle paddle is an awesome mini expedition. It allows you to explore this incredible coastline from the water, getting up close to its wealth of wildlife, history and interesting geology.

LUNAN BAY

Activities	Surfing, paddleboarding, kayaking, swimming
Experience level	★ ★
Environment	Ocean
Start point	Car park behind the dunes
Carry time	5–10 minutes
Public transport	Bus connections from Arbroath
OS map	382

Lunan Bay is one of, if not the finest beach in Angus. Set in a rural, secluded location, this mile-long sandy bay is a brilliant place to soak up some blue health, with a huge number of options for exploring the ocean and undertaking an adventure.

Lunan Bay is situated between the east coast towns of Montrose and Arbroath, and is signposted off the main A92 road. From here you will follow a single-track road past the hamlet of Lunan, the Lunan House Hotel, the campsite and cafe, until you reach a large car park tucked behind the dunes. The cafe is a great option for picking up lunch or a warming coffee, however at present there are no available toilet facilities at this beach.

We arrived at Lunan Bay on an incredibly warm summer day and managed to get one of the last available parking spots on this busy Saturday afternoon. Our worries that the beach was going to be packed soon disappeared, as we emerged from the dunes onto this massive expanse of sand. Even with a full car park, Lunan Bay is so large that it never feels too busy on the sand. The beach itself is split in two halves by the Lunan Burn, which flows through the beach and out to sea, meaning that the more accessible northern end of the bay is usually the busiest.

With the prevailing westerly wind blowing offshore along the east coast on the day we visited, we stuck to the shallows and enjoyed paddling lengths of the beach, avoiding the summertime swimmers. On a calmer day, a more adventurous paddle can be found by following the coastline

north, where you will soon find the ruined Boddin Point Lime Kilns jutting out into the sea, and around its headland the Elephant Rock sea arch. This paddle is a big commitment and a full day out, and should only be attempted by those with good sea-paddling experience.

When the swell arrives, Lunan Bay is one of the east coast's premier surf destinations. Powerful North Sea waves break both left and right along the length of the beach. Lunan Bay has relatively consistent waves, especially during the colder months, and is best surfed on a rising mid to high tide. As mentioned, the prevailing wind swings in from the west; this offshore wind, matched with a north-easterly swell, can provide some top-class surfing and SUP surfing conditions. Do be conscious of rip currents on larger swells, especially at the entrance to Lunan Burn, where the water pulls out pretty fast into the ocean.

In terms of swimming, Lunan Bay is a great place for a chilly North Sea dip throughout the year. During the summer months you will see beach goers, young and old, entering the water here. But during the winter months the water seems to be reserved for only the hardiest local swimmers. Again, do be conscious of rip currents when there is a lot of swell in the bay and the prevailing off-shore wind, especially if you are taking inflatables into the water.

Lunan Bay is a huge expansive beach, a brilliant place to spend a warm summer day with the family or enjoy a bracing winter surf on some top-quality east coast waves.

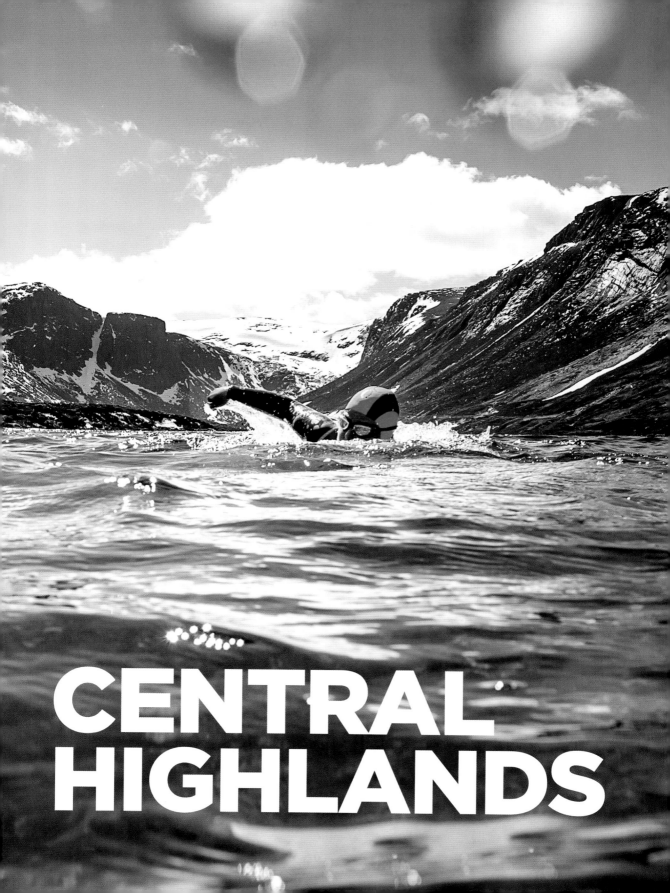

CENTRAL HIGHLANDS

LOCH AN EILEIN

Activities	Paddleboarding, swimming
Experience level	∗
Environment	Freshwater loch
Start point	Car park at Loch an Eilein (charge)
Carry time	5 minutes
Public transport	Train station in Aviemore
OS map	OL 57

Hidden deep between the Scots pine trees at Rothiemurchus is our next blue space, the Loch of the Island, more commonly known as Loch an Eilein. The forest surrounding this picturesque loch is around 1 per cent natural Scots pine, with the remainder extensively re-planted after the Second World War and now lovingly managed by the Rothiemurchus Ranger Service.

Loch an Eilein lies just 5 miles south of Scotland's adventure capital, Aviemore. It is a popular spot for many visitors each year, including watersports enthusiasts, hikers and families. In 2010, Loch an Eilein was even voted Britain's favourite picnic spot!

This coveted loch is popular for good reason, as it has it all. Easy access and parking, a dramatic mountainous backdrop and pine forests reaching down to the water's edge. Loch an Eilein, as you would expect, has an island, which lies just 100 metres from the shore. Steeped in history, it showcases the ruins of a thirteenth-century castle. Over the years this island saw tranquil peace in the shadow of the Cairngorm mountains, but also fierce battles and onslaughts, the most notable being in 1690 when the defeated Jacobites besieged this small castle.

We arrived in early spring, the last of the winter snow still clinging to the Cairngorm mountain range and the snow's meltwater flowing into the loch. This is a brilliant beginner-friendly paddleboarding destination due to its easy access and relative shelter from the surrounding forest.

We pumped up our paddleboards in the large car park and headed down to the water. The loch is extensive and continues far to the south-west, but intrinsically you are drawn straight to the island, the only landmass on the water and an exciting target to reach. It is advised not to land or set foot on the island itself. Many birds use it as a nesting ground, sometimes including ospreys in the summer months.

After paddling around the island a couple of times, exploring the ruins from the safety of our boards, the wind began to pick up. We stuck close to the shoreline for easier paddling and marvelled at the extensive root system of the forest, exposed for all to see and sprawling down to the water's edge.

It is impossible not to be tempted to take a dip under the surface of Loch an Eilein – wild swimming here is also a popular activity. There are many easy access points into the loch from the shore, but it is recommended to use the main beach for water access in order to protect the fragile wildlife habitats along its edge.

After our paddleboarding, I knew I had to take a quick dip; unfortunately, I had forgotten my wetsuit. So I braved the icy meltwater (for a matter of seconds) before retreating to the shore, exhilarated from the frigid dunk.

Loch an Eilein's easy access makes this a relaxed and peaceful option for paddleboarding and swimming in the shadow of the Cairngorm mountain range on a warm summer's afternoon or, in our case, a chilly spring morning.

LOCH MORLICH

Activities	Paddleboarding, kayaking, swimming
Experience level	✴ ✴
Environment	Freshwater loch
Start point	Main beach or parking areas along shore
Carry time	Less than 5 mins
Public transport	Bus connections from Aviemore
OS map	OL 57

With the spectacular backdrop of the northern Cairngorm mountains, which change drastically with the seasons, Loch Morlich is one of Scotland's most accessible freshwater lochs. It is loved and enjoyed by visitors and locals alike, and it is easy to see why. Caledonian pine trees extend down to the water's edge, sandy beaches are scattered along its shore, and Ben Macdui and the great mountain of Cairn Gorm rise on the skyline.

Lying just 6 miles from the hub of Aviemore, it is within easy reach by bike, bus or car. Taking the ski road from Aviemore towards Glenmore Forest Park and the Cairngorms, you will soon see the water's edge on your right-hand side. This road hugs the northern shore of Loch Morlich, with several parking areas along the way with easy launch points on to the water.

At Loch Morlich's north-eastern end, you will find

a beautiful sandy bay that is a must visit for any trip here. This beach is managed by Forestry and Land Scotland and has received awards multiple years in a row from the Keep Scotland Beautiful campaign. It is, in fact, Scotland's only award-winning freshwater beach and the perfect spot to swim at or launch your paddleboard or kayak from.

Here you will also find some great facilities, including toilets, disabled toilets, picnic areas, and information on walking and cycling routes around the loch, as well as Loch Morlich's watersports centre, where you can hire or get lessons on canoes, kayaks, boats and paddleboards.

I have been lucky enough to visit Loch Morlich on many occasions for paddleboarding, swimming, cycling or simply a quick stop off to admire the view en route to the ski centre. On this occasion Rachel and I had been dodging rain showers all day throughout the Cairngorms, so we parked up on the side of the loch and put the kettle on in the van to pass the time while the rain hammered down. It is often said in Scotland, if you don't like the weather, wait 5 minutes and it will change!

Before we had even finished brewing our tea, the clouds parted and bright sun rays shone through. We quickly grabbed our paddleboards and headed onto the loch. The clouds had opened to reveal a scattering of snow on the high mountains. It was late April, so this might potentially have been the last snowfall of the winter. With little wind, the water was glassy calm and we enjoyed a beautiful paddle across to the opposite shore and back before the next rain shower hit.

Loch Morlich is one of those spots that people return to time and time again, finding something new each visit. It is a wonderful spot at any time of year, as it has a way of capturing the seasons in glorious technicolour. In autumn, the leaves start to turn orange and the first flurries of snow settle in the high Cairngorms; the edges of the water often freeze in the winter, with the beaches covered in snow, framed by the towering white mountains; the wildlife begins to stir in the spring, and you can see many young ducklings making their first journeys onto the water; and in the summer the loch is full of outdoors enthusiasts and families making the most of the rare Scottish sun on a sandy beach 300 metres above sea level.

Generations of folk who love the outdoors rate Loch Morlich and we trust them! This popular, accessible watersports destination, with a stunning backdrop, is well worth a visit.

LOCH A'AN (AVON) – CAIRNGORMS NATIONAL PARK

Activities	Swimming
Experience level	✳ ✳ ✳ ✳
Environment	Freshwater loch
Start point	Glenmore lodge
Carry time	4–5 hours each way
Public transport	Train station in Aviemore
OS map	OL 57

Loch A'an, Loch A'an, hoo deep ye lie!
Tell nane yer depth and nane shall I.
Bricht though yer deepmaist pit may be,
Ye'll haunt me till the day I dee.
Bricht, an' bricht, an' bricht as air,
Ye'll haunt me noo for evermair.
> – Nan Shepard, *In The Cairngorms*

Encased on three sides by snow-capped mountains, vertical cliffs and imposing craggy outcrops, Loch A'an is a wonder to experience.

Sometimes known as Loch Avon, this body of water stretches through the valley for nearly 3 miles and is the source of the River Avon. Cairn Gorm, one of Scotland's best-known Munros, rises steeply to

the north, while Ben Macdui, Britain's second-highest mountain, watches over Loch A'an from the south-west.

The remoteness of this loch only adds to its magnificence. Tucked deep within the Cairngorm mountain range, far from any road access, a trip here is reserved for those with an adventurous spirit and sturdy walking boots.

There are multiple routes to reach this loch from various start points in the national park. One of the most spectacular begins at the Cairngorm ski centre, up the famous Goat Track onto the mighty Cairngorm Plateau, and finally descending to the loch via Coire Domhain. This walking route was our plan A. However, a few days before our visit, the Highlands were hit by a huge late-season dump of snow. Without wanting to turn our hopes of a remote wild swim into a full-scale mountaineering expedition, we opted for a low-level approach, avoiding the high, snow-clad tops but adding on a few extra miles.

We parked at Glenmore Lodge, crammed our wetsuits, a stove and some towels into our rucksacks and began the long journey through the Cairngorms. We initially followed the obvious path north-east towards An Lochan Uaine, more affectionately known as 'the Green Lochan'. This spectacular loch, deep turquoise in colour and incredibly enticing, almost tempted us into the water but we knew hiking for the next few hours soaking wet would not be ideal. We averted our gaze and pushed on, our minds fixed on the higher prize of Loch A'an.

After a couple of kilometres, we turned right onto a faint path and followed it close to the meandering River Nethy for kilometre after kilometre. The mountains on either side of us began to slowly rise until soon we were deep in the shady valley known as Strath Nethy.

As if coming to a crescendo, the path steepened and steepened until we finally pulled our tired bodies up over the high point and there it was: Loch A'an in all its glory. From the dark, damp depths of

the Strath Nethy, it felt as if we had topped out into another world.

The snow sticking to the high tops, coupled with the blue sky and wispy clouds, gave it a truly alpine feel. For that moment, it was all worth it. Thoughts of the 4 a.m. alarm, the bog-soaked walking boots and the heavy pack all faded away. We had arrived somewhere truly special.

The loch's water level was very high, meltwater from the peaks having flowed into it during the previous 24-hour thaw. After spotting one of the only beaches visible at this high water, on the north-eastern shore, we headed down to this sandy stretch and prepared for the swim.

This was going to be my coldest swim to date: a 700-metre-high loch filled to bursting with snow meltwater. This then followed by the return four-hour hike to the car! I knew I had to be prepared. I set up my stove, so that as soon as I left the water I would have something warm to eat and drink, essential to avoid my body temperature dropping

too low. I pulled on my wetsuit, socks and high-vis swim bonnet and headed into the icy depths of Loch A'an.

The coldness pricked at every inch of my body, and when I dunked my head underwater the all-too-familiar sensation of brain freeze squeezed at my skull, even with my swim hat on. What proceeded was a type of flailing freestyle technique, with my head poking directly out of the water to avoid another dunking. I finally dropped my ego and resigned myself to breaststroke. However, this technique allowed me to look around in absolute awe and wonder at this location. Towering snowy mountains on every side of me and water clear as glass. Swimming in Loch A'an is an incredibly humbling and awe-inspiring experience; a must for any adventurous wild swimmer.

A trip to Loch A'an necessitates a huge, challenging day in the mountains, but the rewards are there to be reaped with this incredible blue space.

LINN OF TUMMEL

Activities	Swimming, kayaking
Experience level	★ ★ ★ ★
Environment	River
Start point	Linn of Tummel car park
Carry time	5 mins down a steep track
Public transport	N/A; nearest access is Pitlochry
OS map	OL 49

It's easy to forget that you're only a five-minute drive from the roar of the A9 as you swim through the Linn of Tummel. At this point, the slower, meandering River Garry meets the River Tummel just downstream from the Tummel's thundering shallow rapids. Perhaps it's the rush of the white water pouring over rock that drowns out the sound of the nearby road, or else the dense forest absorbs the noise of the traffic.

The Linn of Tummel is a beautiful spot for a swim. We recommend starting from the nearby car park, which was fairly busy the day we visited with several white-water kayakers who had just come off the river. Our knee-jerk response to this was hesitation – surely our swimming spot wouldn't be suitable if it also played host to these sporty kayaks? Nevertheless, we persisted, and it was well worth it.

We headed down the path which curves slightly to the right and runs alongside the water for about 50 metres before an easy-access path appears. Don't let your enthusiasm for a swim cause you to be hasty and try to clamber down to the water too soon; better to wander further on and take the safer route.

As we headed into the water, a group of young

canoeists headed up past us, with their instructor guiding them towards the rapids further up. Their excited shouts were the backdrop to most of our swim, as they jumped into the deep water. *Linne* is the Gaelic origin of 'Linn', which does in fact mean deep water, an accurate description of this area where the two rivers converge.

There are many wild swimming spots in this book that will allow you to slowly absorb the beauty of your surroundings whilst being buoyed along by a gentle flow of water. In comparison, the Linn of Tummel has a slightly stronger current which flows faster on the right-hand side of the river (when looking upstream). We opted to head downstream in the flow, passing close to a footbridge over the River Garry, then swim back up close to the bank protected by a rocky outcrop that reduced the current.

With this in mind, we would highly recommend checking the conditions ahead of time. If the river is in spate, the current is likely to be too strong for swimming. This location is one that should be saved for a clear, dry day. However, in the right circumstances this really is a wonderful swimming spot. Dense, forest-like vegetation towers high above the river on all sides, reaching all the way down to the edge of the water. Ferns and fronds droop over the banks to almost touch the surface. Although we weren't lucky enough to glimpse much wildlife on our visit (perhaps scared off by the enthusiasm of our canoeist friends!) there's the opportunity to spot many different creatures, including red squirrels and otters, nearby.

The Linn of Tummel is a small slice of blue space found in the heart of lush green woodland that makes it feel truly wild.

SOLDIER'S LEAP

Activities	Swimming
Experience level	✳ ✳
Environment	River
Start point	Killiecrankie Visitor Centre
Carry time	20 minutes down a steep set of stairs
Public transport	Bus connections from Blair Atholl
OS map	OL 49

Soldier's Leap at Killiecrankie was not quite the day out I expected it to be. While I was researching for this book, I had seen countless photos and read various stories of a dramatic gap in a high-sided gorge where a Redcoat soldier had fled the pursuing Jacobites by leaping across the River Garry. Make no mistake, it had all the anticipated drama, but it also had an unexpected natural pool slightly downstream that was calm enough for it to be full of small children and families.

My visit to Soldier's Leap was a long time coming. Our first attempt in mid-spring was sadly cut short, as the river was in spate and the conditions were far too dangerous to attempt swimming. Nevertheless, we persisted and I'm very thankful that we returned in early autumn for a second try.

The Killiecrankie car park and visitor centre are easily accessed about 2.5 miles from the A9 in either direction. National Trust for Scotland (NTS) run this location, so the car park does require pay-and-display. However, the visitor centre is free to enter and contains lots of great information about the historical significance of Killiecrankie. There is also a cafe, which provides a great selection of warm food to help you thaw out after a swim. Both the visitor centre and the cafe have seasonal opening hours, so it's worth checking ahead on the NTS website.

The path down to the water is accessed through a covered walkway that runs alongside the visitor centre. From there you follow a steep set of steps that weaves down the side of the hill. There are several signposts pointing towards Soldier's Leap; these lead you to a great viewing point from which you can see the spot where Donald McBane is said to have made his 5.5-metre leap across the river.

To access the water, you must steer in the opposite direction, instead following signs for the Pass of Killiecrankie, which leads you down to the edge of the river. There you will find a large stony beach underneath the towering Killiecrankie Viaduct, where trains frequently pass overhead on what must be a very scenic journey indeed!

The River Garry runs down the west side of the beach, but we would recommend entering the water on the north side towards Soldier's Leap. Here you will find a large pool of water that is kept from becoming stagnant by the continuous flow of the river but is sheltered enough to provide a gentle swimming spot for younger blue space enthusiasts (including our puppy, Sennen, who very hesitantly

followed us into the water). It's beautiful for a swim, surrounded by trees on all sides which were just beginning to turn orange. We also saw several fish leaping from the water nearby.

More confident swimmers can head from here upstream towards Soldier's Leap. The river narrows as the sides of the gorge grow steeper above it, and as I swam against the gentle current I thought often of how terrifying it must have been to leap across the gap. Luckily, I didn't have to imagine for too long – once we had made it up the gorge, we did a depth test and discovered that the river was far deeper than we could jump, meaning it was safe to make a leap.

We didn't follow in Donald McBane's footsteps, however; instead, we stood on top of the towering stones and jumped into the river. This was still an intimidating feat – even knowing we had a safe landing awaiting us and with no Jacobites on our tail! After this, the swim back to the beach was much easier, as we went with the flow of the river, which quickly carried us back.

Soldier's Leap and Killiecrankie Gorge are a small investment for a high return adventure, with a well-marked path leading down to a beautiful pool surrounded by woodland and a river packed with history flowing through. Well worth the trip!

ADVENTURE PLANNING & SAFETY

SAFETY BASICS

All the activities included in *Blue Scotland* – paddleboarding, kayaking, surfing and wild swimming – should be approached with caution, as spending time in blue spaces can come with risks. These can be reduced, and it is advised to do your own research as well as undertaking professional training in addition to what is included here in order to ensure your safety and the safety of others around you.

These are some of the fundamental principles that we employed whilst researching for this book:

Know your limits
- Stay within your ability and do not feel pressured to step outside your comfort zone. As the saying goes, *if in doubt, stay out*, meaning if you're not sure of the conditions or your ability, then don't go in.

Safety in numbers
- Always go with a friend; even better, two friends.
- Always tell someone where you're going, what you will be doing and what time you anticipate being back.

Know your group
- What experience do they have? Can they rescue themselves and can they rescue other people? What safety equipment are they carrying and do they know how to use it? Do they have any medical conditions you should know about?

Plan your trip and route
- Check the weather, visibility, tides and swell (see p. 209). Calculate your timings based on distance and speed.
- Think about potential hazards along your route and where the exit points could be in case of an emergency.
- Continuously monitor the conditions and adjust your plans accordingly.

Clothing
- Wear appropriate clothing for the environment you will be in. Dress for immersion and be aware of water temperature.
- Wear a buoyancy aid when kayaking and paddleboarding.

Equipment
- Check your equipment for damage before leaving home and repair if necessary.
- Always carry a means of communication and keep it in reach and dry at all times.
- Dress appropriately for the water temperature, which in Scotland stays low year round.

Skills and ability
- Undertake professional training in your chosen watersport from qualified organisations and individuals.

TIDES

There is nothing more natural than the reliable rise and fall of the ocean's tides. As someone who uses Scotland's blue spaces, the tide is an important phenomenon to understand, to always check before entering the water and around which to curate your adventure plans. It is well worth taking a tidal planning course, which can be done in a classroom or online.

The tide is caused by the gravitational pull of the moon and, to a lesser extent, the sun. In Scotland, a low tide and a high tide will occur twice each day at all locations, with the high and low tides being approximately six hours apart. The tide times are not the same each day, neither is the actual height of high and low tide.

Spring tides & neap tides

Spring tides occur approximately every two weeks at full moon and new moon, whereas neap tides occur on the half moons, seven days after a spring tide.

Spring tides are when the tidal range between high tide and low tide are at their maximum, and neap tides are when this range is at its minimum.

The most important thing to note for blue-space users is that during a spring tide currents and tidal flow are stronger than on neap tides. This is because more water has to flow between high and low tide over the same six-hour period, making it flow faster – approximately twice as fast on a spring tide as on a neap tide.

Tidal flow

The speed of tidal flow changes dramatically during the ebb and flood of a tide. It is important to understand that more water moves during the middle two hours of an incoming tide and an outgoing tide; this is when currents are at their strongest.

Do note that tidal-flow rates can be very complicated and localised, meaning it is always important to seek local knowledge.

Rip currents

In the UK, the majority of RNLI lifeguard incidents involve rip currents. A rip current is a specific type of current that occurs from a beach with breaking waves – usually the larger the swell, the faster and larger the rip currents are, but do be aware that rip currents can also be experienced on smaller swell days.

A rip current is a strong current that runs straight out to sea. Water users can easily be caught in rip currents. If you get stuck in one, it is important not to swim against it; you will quickly get exhausted. Instead, swim parallel to the shore until you are out of the channel of the rip current and then head into shore.

Rip currents can sometimes be hard to spot; it is always advised to spend a few moments scanning a shoreline before entering the water. Rip currents are characterised as a channel of churning, choppy water on the sea's surface, often with fewer waves breaking in this area.

Weather

Scotland's weather can change incredibly quickly on the coast and inland. What starts off as a calm, sunny day can quickly change to a windy and rainy one. It is therefore important to check the weather regularly in the run up to, and even during, an adventure.

An increase in wind can turn a safe situation into a dangerous one. Wind has the ability to very quickly blow a paddleboard out to sea or across a loch. It is very important to not go paddleboarding with a strong offshore wind.

Experiencing rain and cold is very likely while adventuring in Scotland; there is the potential for your body temperature to drop and in the worst case it becomes hypothermic. To avoid this, it is important to invest in good quality kit, know your limits and always have a back-up plan. The water temperature can be chilly in summer and incredibly cold in winter.

Sunburn and sun exhaustion do, in fact, affect water-users in Scotland, more often than you would expect! On a warm summer's day it is important to respect the power of the sun, cover up and wear sun cream.

Lightning storms can also potentially occur, especially during the summer months. If one is forecast, don't head out into a blue space, and if one begins whilst you are on the water, you must get to land quickly and find a safe space.

Water quality

In general, the water quality of blue spaces in the UK is better than it has been for 150 years. This includes the rivers, lochs and beaches. However, it is important to be aware of a couple of water-quality issues.

The first is pollution. This can be from sewage, farm run-off or industrial pollution – all are exacerbated by heavy rain. In some locations it is advised not to swim or enter the water after heavy rain or storms.

The second is blooms of blue-green algae. These can appear on still bodies of inland water during the warm summer months. This algae is best avoided at all costs; it can cause rashes and bad skin reactions for humans, but can be fatal for dogs.

SCOTLAND'S OUTDOOR ACCESS CODE

Scotland enjoys some of the best access rights in the world for outdoor recreation, including water-sports. Access to the outdoors in Scotland is encouraged for visitors and locals alike, as long as it is conducted in a respectful way.

The Scottish Outdoor Access Code is based on three key principles:

1. Respect the interests of others: Being respectful of privacy, peace of mind and safety.

2. Care for the environment: Leave the area you visit as you found it. Or better yet, improve it through litter picks.

3. Take responsibility for your own actions: Caring for your own safety is paramount, be aware of and fully educated on natural hazards and risks.

More advice on the Scottish Outdoor Access Code can be found at www.outdooraccess-scotland.scot.

RESPONSIBLE AND SUSTAINABLE ADVENTURING

Being a responsible and sustainable adventurer is more important now than ever. The Climate Emergency and nature loss are the greatest threats facing the human population and, here in Scotland, we are seeing the impact already.

The effect of the Climate Emergency on biodiversity in Scotland is already devastating: 11 per cent of our species are facing extinction and 25 per cent of our wildlife has already been lost. We all have to do our part to tackle this Climate Emergency at home and while out exploring our blue spaces.

Here are six considerations for the environment that we kept front of mind whilst researching this book:

Consider public transport

This guide provides public transport information for each location. Scotland has great rail, bus and ferry networks, extending to all corners of the country.

Be a conscious consumer

Shop for your outdoor equipment and clothing with the planet in mind. Be conscious of where your products come from, what they are made of and the effect their production has on the planet. There are a growing number of eco-conscious outdoor brands on the market who would love your support.

Support local communities

Shop, eat, drink and invest within local communities. This will allow small, rural businesses to flourish. Across Scotland you will find many local community-led environmental initiatives, including sanitary installation, habitat protection and wildlife education, so do support these with your respect and donations.

Respect the landscape

Whilst in the Scottish outdoors, it is crucial that you do not disturb or damage surrounding landscapes, as many are home to wildlife habitats and protected plant species. Stick to paths and tracks where possible. Be conscious of the natural world, even down to the smallest ecosystems: they all play a role in our survival. Tread lightly on Scotland.

Leave no trace

An important principle across the whole of the Scottish outdoors. Leave the environment as you found it, or better yet, take a spare bin bag with you on an adventure and pick up litter as you go.

Know your limits

The Scottish outdoors is a wonder to explore, but it comes with inherent risk. It is imperative to stay within your limits and get yourself fully educated on your chosen sport and the environment you are entering.

FINAL THOUGHTS

From the tops of its highest mountains to the depths of its deepest lochs, Scotland's natural environment is a wonder to behold and a real privilege to spend time immersed in.

Scotland has accessible blue spaces near every city, town, village and small hamlet. Some are mind-blowingly stunning, some are wild and alive, and others are calm and inviting. Time spent in, on and close to blue spaces has been proven to be good for our minds and bodies by generations of water enthusiasts, and now by scientists too.

I hope you enjoy exploring Scotland's blue spaces as much as I have. I only ask that you respect and preserve the environments we love whilst you soak up some of the blue health benefits on offer.

ACKNOWLEDGEMENTS

This book would not have been possible without the skill, resilience and support of *Blue Scotland*'s photographer, Rachel Keenan. Rachel was part of every adventure in this book, skilfully balancing on her paddleboard and plunging into freezing water to take the incredible photos. Her dedication to the project was inspiring and I will be forever grateful for her friendship.

Thank you to everyone who joined us on a *Blue Scotland* adventure: Owen Connolly, Stevie Boyle from Ocean Vertical, Andreas Heinzl from Unexplored Scotland, the team at Jerba Campervans, Charlotte Workman and Steve Small from the Adventure Photographers, Kaitlin McKenzie, and Sennen, my adventure pup.

My final thanks go to my partner Tegan, for believing in this project, for your unconditional support, for going wild swimming when I thought it was too cold and for being a sounding board at every stage of this project.

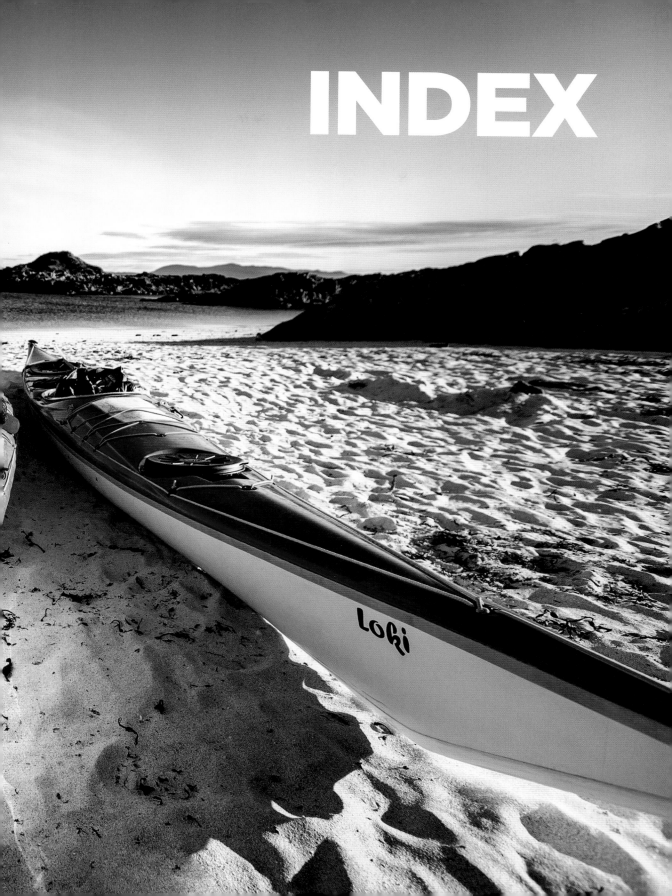

INDEX

Aberdeen 180–1
Achmelvich Bay 148–51
Adventure Photographers 58
Antarctica 10, 24
Ardlui 55
Ardnish Peninsula 88
Arisaig 84–8
Arisaig Skerries 84–7
Armadillo 48
Arrochar 54–7
Arrochar Pier 55
Aviemore 190–2

Balnakeil Beach 155
Barnbougle Castle 21
Barra (Isle of) 116–19
    Barra Airport 119
    Castlebay and Kisimuil Castle 116–17
    Traigh Eais & Traigh Mhor 118–19
Bass Rock 29
Beinn Eighe Nature Reserve 74
Belhaven Bay 28
Belhaven Surf Centre 29
Ben Lomond 54, 58
Benbecula 122–3
    Peter's Port 122–3
Berwick-upon-Tweed 30
Blackhouse Watersports (Tiree) 106
black-throated diver 80
blue health 12
Bonnie Prince Charlie 80, 88, 120–1
Bow Fiddle Rock 170–3
Bridges of the Forth 32–5

Cairngorms National Park 196–8
Calbha (Iona) 105
Calgary Bay 102–3
Castlebay 116–17
Castle Pool, St Andrews 43
Castle Tioram 82–3
Ceannabeinne Beach 155
Central Belt 50
Coldingham Bay 30
Cramond Beach 20
Cramond Island 20
Cullykhan Bay 178–9

Dalmeny Estate 20–1, 22
Dark Sky Community 108
dolphins 31, 103, 117, 139, 143, 160
Dumfries 70–1
Dunbar 28
Dunnet Beach 160–1

Dunnottar Castle 182, 184–5
Durness 154–5

Eas Fors Waterfall 100
Easdale Island 94–7
East Links Family Park 29
East Lothian 24–8
East Neuk 40
Edinburgh 20–1, 22–3, 32–3, 50, 51
Eilean Donan Castle 78–9
Ellenabeich 94–5
Eriskay 120–1
    Prince's Strand 120–1

Falkirk 50, 52
Falkirk Wheel 50–1
Fidden Beach 98–9
Fidra Island 24–6
Fife 36–40
Finnieston Crane 48
Fionnphort 104
Firth of Forth 22, 33, 60
Forth Bridge 32
Forth and Clyde Canal 50–1
Forth Road Bridge 32

Galloway 70–1
Galloway and Southern Aryshire
    Biosphere 70
Glasgow 44, 46, 48, 50, 54, 56
Glasgow to Edinburgh Canoe Trail 50–1
Glenfinnan 80
Glenlee 48
golden eagle 80
Granton 22
Grey Mare's Tail 66–8
grey seals 31
guillemots 24, 150, 185

Handa Island 153
Harris (Isle of) 130, 134, 136, 138
    Scarista 130–1
    Luskentyre 134–5
    Huisinis 136–7
    Traigh Mheilein 138–9
Harry Potter 80
Hell's Lum 178–9
Hosta (North Uist) 124–5
Huisinis (Harris) 136–7

Iona 104
    Calbha Beach 105
    Port Ban 105

Jacobites 80
John Muir 28–9
John Muir Country Park 28

kayaking 14, 54, 82, 84, 88, 116
Kelpies, The 52
Kilchurn Castle 64–5
Kinghorn Loch 36
Kisimul Castle 116–17

Lake of Menteith 62–3
Leith 22
Lewis (Isle of) 140–1
    Traigh Ghearadha 140–1
Linn of Tummel 200–01
Loch A'an (Avon) 196
Loch Alsh 78–9
Loch an Eilein 190–1
Loch Ard 58, 60–1
Loch Awe 64–5
Loch Duich 78–9
Loch Ken 70–1
Loch Lomond 54–6
Loch Lomond & the Trossachs National Park
    54, 56, 58, 62
Loch Long 78–9
Loch Maree 74–5, 77
Loch Moidart 82–3
Loch Morar 90–1
Loch Morlich 192–93
Loch Ness 164–7
Loch Ore 38
Lochore Meadows Country Park 38
Loch Roe 151
Loch Shiel 80
Loch Skeen 67–8
Long Craig Rocks 28
Lunan Bay 186–7
Luskentyre (Harris) 134–5
Luss 55

minke whale 31, 143
Moffat 66
Mount Everest 10
Mull (Isle of) 98–104
    Calgary Bay 102–3
    Eas Fors Waterfall 100–1
    Fidden Beach 98–9

North Berwick 26
North Coast 500 148
North Coast Watersports 161

North Uist 124–28
    Hosta 124–5
    Scolpaig 126–7
    Sollas 128–9

Ocean Vertical 11, 24

Peanmeanach Bothy 88
peregrine falcon 80
Peter's Port (Benbecula) 122
Port Ban (Iona) 105
Portnellan Organic Farm 54
Prince's Strand (Eriskay) 120–1
puffins 24

Queensferry Crossing 32

razorbills 24
River Clyde 46
River Forth 60
Riverside Museum 46, 48
RNLI lifeguarded beaches 28
Rob Roy 60–1
RSPB Nature Reserves 24, 74

St Andrews 40–3
St Columba 104
St Kilda 142–5
St Vedas Surf Shop 30
Sandend Bay 174–7
Sango Bay 155
Scarista (Harris) 130–3
Scolpaig (Harris) 126–7
Scotland's Outdoor Access Code 211
Scottish Canals 50
Scourie Bay 152–3
seals 26, 48, 79, 84, 86, 117, 133, 151, 152, 161
Skye (Isle of) 78–9
Slate Quarries 94–7
Slatterdale 75
Slioch 75
Smoo Cave 154
Solider's Leap 202–3
Sollas (North Uist) 128–9
South Pole 10, 24
South Queensferry 32
South Uist 120–1
Stevenson, Robert Louis 24
Stonehaven 182–5
Strathy Beach 156–7

Thurso 158, 160

Thurso East 158–9
tidal pool 43, 126, 178
tides 211
Tiree 106–8
    Balevullin Beach 106
    Gott Bay 108
Traigh a Bhaigh 115
Traigh Eais (Barra) 118–19
Traigh Ghearadha (Lewis) 140–1
Traigh Mheilein (Harris) 138–9
Traigh Mhor (Barra) 118–19
Traigh Shiar (Vatersay)
Treasure Island 24

Unexplored Scotland 83, 87
Union Canal 50–1

Vatersay 112, 115
    Traigh Shiar 115
    Traigh a Bhaigh 115

Wardie Bay 22
Wave Classic (Tiree) 106
Waverley 46–7
Whaligoe Steps 162–3
white-tailed sea eagle 80
windsurfing 106–7

Yellowcraig Beach 24